EAT
CLEAN
LIVE
WELL

EAT CLEAN LIVE WELL

TERRY WALTERS

Photography by Julie Bidwell

STERLING EPICURE
New York

STERLING EPICURE
New York

An Imprint of Sterling Publishing
387 Park Avenue South
New York, NY 10016

Designed by MacKenzie Brown Design
Chicago, Illinois
www.mackenziebrown.com

Photography by Julie Bidwell
West Hartford, Connecticut

ISBN 978-1-4027-7927-5

Library of Congress Cataloging-in-Publication Data Available

Distributed in Canada by Sterling Publishing
c/o Canadian Manda Group, 165 Dufferin Street
Toronto, Ontario, Canada M6K 3H6
Distributed in the United Kingdom by GMC Distribution Services
Castle Place, 166 High Street, Lewes, East Sussex, England BN7 1XU
Distributed in Australia by Capricorn Link (Australia) Pty. Ltd.
P.O. Box 704, Windsor, NSW 2756, Australia

For information about custom editions, special sales, and premium and corporate purchases,
please contact Sterling Special Sales at 800-805-5489 or specialsales@sterlingpublishing.com.

Manufactured in Canada

10 9 8 7 6 5 4 3 2 1

www.sterlingpublishing.com

Dedicated with love
to Chip, Sarah and Sydney.
You are my every reason.

This clean food journey...

has changed my life in ways I never could have imagined. What started as an interest in eating clean and living well has evolved into a passion that inspires me every day. And from it has grown a community that nourishes me and fills me with purpose, belonging and love. There are too many people to name individually, but the energy and spirit of each one is reflected within the pages of this book. My deepest gratitude to all of you—always in my heart as I write, cook, explore, learn and live.

Walking through the greenhouses and fields of Urban Oaks Organic Farm in New Britain, Connecticut centers me and ignites my creativity and passion. A Friday afternoon at the farm is like wrapping up the week with a gift. There have been many whose friendships I value, but I owe Farmer Mark Rutkowski, Mariana Evica and Victor Blanco special thanks for their support through the making of this book. And for Mike Kandefer, founding farmer and dear friend, who puts every plant and person before himself, there are no words to express my gratitude.

It is an honor to be part of The Institute of Sustainable Nutrition—to work with Allison and Nigel, to share the kitchen with these passionate and thoughtful students and to call its founder, Joan Palmer, my teacher and my friend.

To Tony Camilleri, my partner in crime creating healthy school lunch programs. How rewarding (and fun) it is to work beside you in the kitchen.

Thanks to farmers and friends Rodger and Isabelle Phillips of Sub Edge Farm, Haley and Andy Billipp of Eddy Farm and Belltown Hill Orchard for allowing me to photograph the land you so beautifully cultivate. And thanks to Peggy Hall and everyone at the Hill-Stead and Norfolk Farmers Markets who welcomed me (and my photographer).

There are friends, and then there are running partners. Part family, part therapist and always there for me at the end of the driveway, whether it's 80° or -8°. Sue Davies and Meara McCarthy—thank you for keeping me going strong.

Thank you for your love and support these past months and always—Gary Jacobs, Allison Bauer and Barbara Gadd.

To my entire Sterling Publishing family, past and present, and especially Theresa Thompson, Jennifer Williams, Blanca Oliviery and Caitlin Friedman, my sincere thanks for your support.

To my agent, Tony Gardner, my heartfelt thanks for your unwavering support and friendship.

To photographer, Julie Bidwell, with whom I have spent the better part of this past year. And to food stylist Maria Sacasa, thank you not only for documenting my clean food journey, but for being part of this ECLW adventure.

The MacKenzie Brown Design team that created this and all of my books is like none other. To Pete Kowalski, if only you could retouch me every time I walk out the door! And to Kurt MacKenzie and Andrew Brown, who make me laugh every day and love every minute of these projects. You have outdone yourselves again. Thank you seems hardly enough.

Change hats, Mr. Brown, because this one is personal. Another book, another chapter, but always my best friend.

To my parents, who set the bar high for healthy living and parenting, and share infinite grace, wisdom, friendship and love.

To my girls, Sarah and Sydney, who bring meaning to every day. My heart overflows with love and pride.

And to Chip, who stands beside me every step of the way, tasting every recipe, washing every dish, and providing endless support to allow me to follow my heart and chase my dreams. I love you.

Contents

Not a mealtime goes by that the lessons my mother taught me aren't clearly evident. The symphony of ... l tastes she prepared and served with love ...ted in my own home-cooked meals and ...y family with wholesome nourishment. ...th and wellbeing today requires greater ...t did in years past. While I do my best to ...y family and myself, our mealtime today ...e I experienced and relished as a child.

...vas to ...th ...essed, ...s we all ...tein, an ...ariety of ...cleaner ...er we ...oday, ...and our ...ich more. ...t and ...whether ...se or ...g us ...to good ...choices, ...of stress ...ay. ...nience ...we are ...now. ...sses than ...products ...ating our ...With ...rtant, we	respond with even more extremes, grasping for health and balance that will never be found in a pill, a fad diet or a marketing statement. The answer is always the same—a varied, clean food diet. But the further we stray from this path, the more challenging the journey.

I am forever inspired by the wisdom and passion of those around me, and convinced that by sharing this journey we can achieve undeniable movement and progress toward establishing a more sustainable future. I hope that my story resonates with you in some way, but even more importantly, that it helps inspire your own story, grounded in a bounty of clean food and nourished by the activities and rituals connected with the changing seasons. Use this information to help guide you along a path that supports the good health of our communities, our environment, our future and ourselves.

EAT CLEAN LIVE WELL is about making the choices that give beauty and meaning to each day and allow us to live with intention, purpose and good health. |

The Changing Landscape of Clean Food

Our family's shared meals, my weekly trips to the farm and visits to farmers markets remind me of how food brings us together. But our adulterated food system, the politics influencing it and so much uncertainty around truly sustainable, healthy food reveal the reality of how deeply food divides us as well. Our food system is polluting our bodies and our environment, and the negative affects of over-processing our food and the land that produces it are everywhere, from dwindling natural resources to our deteriorating health.

Two engines drive our food system. One is a profit-based business and political model that does not always have our best interest at heart. This model is in part a response to our demands for products that fill short-term needs (a picky child, busy schedule or waning energy), but create long-term imbalance and disease. In contrast, the second engine is fueled by the growing clean food movement that is helping to sustain small farms and provide an essential connection to the source of our food.

Perhaps the only thing we know for certain is that food is ever-changing in ways good and bad. New pesticides and herbicides, advancements in genetic modification, depletion of the soil and relaxed organic standards are not transparent to consumers at the point of purchase and come with the potential for great risks to our health. Large single-crop farms (monocultures) deplete the nutrient density of soil, threaten crop diversity, are more vulnerable to insects and disease, and put our food and water supplies at risk.

At the same time, more and more people are participating in gardening, the number of small farms continues to rise, and special programs and grants are making clean food more accessible. Schoolyard gardens are increasingly common, while nutrition and cooking education are being brought back into the classroom as well.

Unlike my mother, I don't prepare dinner from scratch every night. Sometimes "upcycling" the previous night's dinner into a new dish or having my children prepare the meal is the only way mealtime happens. Sitting down to share a meal is always a gift and sometimes a luxury. But the greatest difference between the meals in my mother's kitchen and mine is the dialogue about food—where it comes from, how it was grown or produced, and how it influences our health, our community, our environment and even our world.

In my mother's kitchen, I ate with blind faith. Today, I want to know the land, the farmer, the fisherman, the grocer and all the processes from seed to plate to ensure that the food on my table will nourish and not harm.

The more we insist upon clean food options and knowing the truth behind the label, the more demand we'll create for the foods and food system that are in balance with the rhythm of the seasons and which sustain good health.

BUILDING HEALTHY COMMUNITIES

There I stood, before 200 high school students, teaching them what it means to eat clean and why they should demand clean food in their school cafeteria, when one student shouted out, "Why is your generation always telling my generation to fix this problem?"

Creating healthy change in our food system and our communities will not come from one generation telling another what has to be done, but rather from all of us joining our voices and actions to make it happen each and every day.

We can all make changes individually that will positively influence our health, but it will take all of us coming together to create healthy communities. With more access to seasonal fresh foods through farms, farmers markets and food hubs; nutrition and cooking education through schools and community centers; wellness programs and outreach to all ages, we gain not only healthy communities, but invaluable connections to each other and the land.

You never know what will inspire positive change. It can come from an organization, a teacher, an event and even the most resistant child, who in one minute is disgusted by the very thought of kale in a smoothie, and is encouraging all of his peers to drink it along with him in the next. It can require hard work to open minds and create opportunity, and sometimes it just requires working hands and caring hearts.

Clean Food Kids

When my children were younger, we would go to the farm and to the dump every week. Over time, they learned that everything comes from someplace, everything goes someplace, and that they play a key role in that cycle. I don't force my children to eat well, but I do make sure to provide them with healthy options. And since we know that our children learn as much (if not more) from what we do than from what we say, I teach by example and talk about the choices I'm making in order to empower and inspire them to make healthy choices for themselves.

As a mom, I can't help but want to meet my children's every need and protect them from every consequence. But when I let go of the need to get good food into their bodies and focus on teaching about clean food and what a healthy meal looks like, I start to see results (and life becomes a lot easier).

To this day, my goal is for food to nourish my family and bring us together, rather than harm or divide us. I prepare one meal, but honor the likes and dislikes of everyone in the family. I always make sure there is at least something for everyone, even if I'm presenting something new. Here are some of the practices I use to encourage everyone in my family to be adventurous and healthy eaters.

Talk about clean food and healthy choices. Eating clean means bringing in a rainbow of color and all five tastes (sweet, salty, sour, bitter and pungent); knowing where food comes from; learning to read and understand labels; and eating foods that come from a green plant and not a processing plant.

Set some ground rules. In our home, you have to at least try new foods. If you don't like them, you don't have to eat them, but you do have to try them again if they're prepared differently and served a few months down the road. You never know when your tastes are going to change!

Make it fun! As soon as children realize you have an agenda, they'll be on to you and will be more likely to resist change. Focus on making it fun and educational each day. Get everyone involved in menu planning, shopping, cooking, setting the table and, most definitely, cleaning up.

Serve family style. It's human nature to resist things that are forced upon us. Nobody likes having a heaping pile of expectations dropped on their plate! Children and adults alike are often more open to trying new foods (and even taking seconds) when they can serve themselves. This also teaches children to listen to their bodies and serve their unique constitution and needs.

Join a CSA (Community Supported Agriculture). Purchasing a share of a local farm's harvest is a fun way to teach kids about clean food, make an adventure out of trying a bounty of seasonal produce, connect with the source of your food and support your local farmer and food system. Picking up your share can be a memorable and educational family outing, especially if your farm allows you to pick your own produce, feed the animals and cut your own flowers.

Reduce temptation. Fill your pantry with healthy options and leave the indulgences behind. Make the hard choices, once at the grocery store, so that you aren't faced with making them every time you open your cupboard.

Wrap it up! Make trying new veggies simple, fun and delicious by serving them in tacos, burritos, summer-roll wrappers and even smoothies. Better yet, put everything out on the table and let kids make their own.

Make snacks mini meals. Follow the same clean food guidelines for snacking as you would for any other meal—offer a rainbow of color and all five tastes, minimally processed for maximum nutrition. Healthy snacks can be easy to grab when you keep fruit, cut up vegetables, dips, and prepared foods on hand, instead of non-nutritional and even harmful junk food. Stock your pantry with healthy clean food so you don't have to say no to unhealthy options (play the role of the cruise director, not the police).

Add new clean foods to foods kids already love. Adding one new vegetable to soup, pasta or salad is a great way to introduce foods and develop a taste for something without being overwhelmed by it. I also like to pump up the nutritional value of a recipe by adding healthy ingredients—even if it means sneaking them in. Just be sure to come clean eventually. No child is well served believing that mommy's Blondies, for instance, are the same as any other Blondie when, in actuality, they are made with almond meal and cannellini beans!

Plant a garden. Gardens make perfect classrooms for teaching about food and nutrition, the cycles of life, the seasons, the environment, responsibility, working together, patience and so much more. From selecting and planting seeds, to watering, weeding and eventually harvesting, gardens allow us to be invested in and connected to our food, while providing limitless learning and bonding. Best of all, children are more likely to eat and enjoy the fruits of their own labor.

Serve love. Separate cooking from the rest of your day. Take a deep breath, exhale tension and stress, and focus on cooking love into your meals.

Be grateful. Give thanks for the delicious food on the plate, the nutrition it provides, the hands that prepared it, the farmer who grew it, and the soil, sun and water that allowed it to grow.

Compost. From the food we eat to the water we drink to the packages we discard, consumerism has a profound impact on our health as well as the health of our communities, environment, economy and future. Turning food scraps into nutrition for our soil supports a healthy food system and reduces waste.

Sharing clean food and healthy living with children extends far beyond simply getting good food into their bodies. Parenting challenges us to provide our children with the tools and knowledge to make healthy choices, but it is even harder to then let go and hope that they will be inspired to use what we have taught them. Whether our children make healthy choices or not does not determine our success as parents. In the end, nourishment from sharing mealtimes and healthy parent-child relationships are gifts that easily trump the small battles over finishing what's on the plate.

Clean Food Basics

Eating clean is about nourishing yourself with food grown from the earth, in harmony with the seasons and environment, and minimally processed for maximum nutrition. For every truth we know about nutrition, another truth is challenged every day. Inherently, we know that good health will not come from a promise on a label or a trend that does not honor our unique constitution. Rather, it will come from filling our plates with a variety of whole foods, all cooked with love. Here's how.

THE CLEAN FOOD PANTRY

Set yourself up for success by stocking up on the foods you'll need to make a variety of clean food recipes. Plan in advance, make a shopping list and pick one new clean recipe to try each week. Each time you make a new recipe you'll likely purchase one or two ingredients that will be new to your pantry, as well. In just a couple of months, you'll have your own clean food pantry and will have made a slow and successful transition to clean foods that are perfectly suited to your tastes and health, not to mention your budget! Focus on bringing in healthy new foods and over time, the unhealthy foods that weren't serving you will be reduced, or fall by the wayside completely.

The following list is not intended to be comprehensive, but rather a good place to start so that you'll have most of the ingredients needed to make the recipes in this book. Keep a rotating supply of grains, legumes, nuts and seeds in mason jars in your pantry so that you'll be ready to make a variety of healthy meals and menus.

CONDIMENTS
sea salt (fine and coarse), pepper, extra virgin olive oil, virgin coconut oil, mirin (brown rice cooking wine), apple cider vinegar, red wine vinegar, balsamic vinegar, ume plum vinegar

WHOLE GRAINS
brown rice, millet, quinoa, rolled oats (gluten-free)

LEGUMES
black beans, cannellini beans, chickpeas, lentils, pinto beans, split peas

NUTS, SEEDS AND BUTTERS
almonds, cashews, pecans, walnuts, pumpkin seeds, sesame seeds, sunflower seeds

HERBS AND SPICES
cayenne, chile, cinnamon, cumin, curry, mustard seeds, oregano, paprika, thyme, turmeric

FOR BAKING
baking powder, baking soda, almond meal, teff flour, millet flour, arrowroot, coconut milk, applesauce, maple syrup

MISCELLANEOUS
dried mushrooms, dried sea vegetables (kombu, nori, wakame, arame), grapeseed oil mayonnaise, miso, sundried tomatoes, tamari, vegetable stock

PRODUCE
A selection of seasonal fresh produce, plus garlic, onions, carrots, celery, kale, salad greens, lemons (lemon juice), ginger root and turmeric root

MENU PLANNING

Each week I select the best locally grown produce offered at the best price (whether from the farm or grocery store) and plan my meals from there. With a well-stocked pantry and a few basics, there are always plenty of options for breakfast, lunch and dinner. Here are some strategies I use to decrease the stress of making healthy meals and increase my success.

Start with fresh produce. Mother Nature gives us what we need when we need it. Seasonal produce is more likely to be locally grown, in ample supply, freshly picked, better tasting and more reasonably priced.

Select recipes to make during the week. Create a shopping list so you have everything you need for the recipes you want to prepare. Then fill your cart the rest of the way with fresh vegetables, fruit and any needed staples. I keep a chalkboard in the kitchen so family members can write down items they want or that need to be replenished, and check the list before heading to the store.

Set aside time to cook. Some people prefer to make meals for the whole week all at once; others prefer to do their cooking every few days. Figure out what works best for you and then stick to your plan.

Make a habit of bedtime food prep. Use the time before you go to bed to review your menus and prepare. Put the next morning's oatmeal in a pot with water to soak overnight so that it takes less time to cook in the morning; place the next night's grains or legumes in water to soak; and wrap up leftovers to eat for lunch the next day.

Cook in quantity. Cook multiple servings and store leftovers in an airtight container in the refrigerator. For instance, make a large container of chia pudding for multiple breakfasts and ferment several bottles of kraut or radishes at one time, so you put the effort in once and get back many servings with no additional effort.

Upcycle your food. All it takes to turn last night's leftover roasted vegetables into tomorrow's roasted vegetable soup is a little stock and a handheld blender. Turn those same vegetables into pâté by blending them in a food processor and seasoning them to taste with herbs and spices. Upcycle cooked grains into grain salads by tossing them with chopped vegetables, olive oil and vinegar. Wrap up leftovers in a burrito, summer roll or a sheet of nori, or use them to top a toasted rice tortilla for a personalized crispy pizza.

Keep track. Use the "Notes" pages in the back of this book to write down your menus, favorite themes for meals, sources for foods and supplies, the phone number for the local CSA and the hours when your farmers market is in full swing. Write directly on the pages of each recipe to note your variations, tips and thoughts. Tag pages of recipes you want to try and especially those you already know you love.

Share the journey. Friends and family members can make your clean eating efforts that much more successful and nourishing, whether you're just starting or are far along in your journey. Share recipe ideas, food prep, meals, trips to the farmers market and even a plot at the community garden and appreciate the added support and fun when you don't have to go it alone.

COOKING GRAINS AND BEANS

Mastering these basic cooking techniques will make meal prep especially quick and easy.

Soaking grains and beans for a minimum of one hour washes away phytic acid which draws minerals from the body. It also brings grains and beans closer to germination, which unlocks their nutritional value and makes them easier to digest. Finally, adding kombu infuses them with minerals and reduces gaseous properties.

BROWN RICE, LENTILS, QUINOA (red and black)
1   cup rice, lentils or quinoa
2   cups water or stock
Thumb-size piece of kombu or pinch of sea salt

IVORY QUINOA
1   cup quinoa
1½ cups water or stock
Thumb-size piece of kombu or pinch of sea salt

WILD RICE, WHOLE OATS, SPLIT PEAS
1   cup rice, whole oats or peas
2½ cups water or stock
Thumb-size piece of kombu or pinch of sea salt

Place grains, lentils or split peas in pot with enough water to cover and soak at least 1 hour. Transfer to mesh basket, rinse and drain. Return to pot, add water or stock, kombu or salt, and bring to boil. Reduce heat and simmer covered until liquid is absorbed. Remove from heat, cool slightly before fluffing to keep grains from becoming mushy, and serve or add to recipe as instructed.

NOTE: Presoak grains or beans, rinse and add to stainless steel rice cooker with water or stock, and kombu or salt. Cover, turn on rice cooker and it will turn off automatically when done.

MILLET
1   cup millet
1   cup water or stock
Pinch of sea salt

Millet doesn't require presoaking but benefits from toasting to bring out its nutty flavor. Rinse in mesh basket and drain. Heat Dutch oven to medium heat and add millet. Toast, stirring continuously, until dry and fragrant (3-4 minutes). Add water or stock and sea salt, and simmer covered 25 minutes or until liquid is absorbed. Remove from heat, cool slightly before fluffing, and serve or add to recipe as instructed.

BEANS
I cook beans with more liquid than needed so they roll as they boil and cook more evenly.

1   cup dried beans
6   cups water
Sea salt
Thumb-size piece of kombu

Place dry beans in pot and cover with 3 inches of water. Soak 6 hours or overnight, drain and rinse. In pot, bring water to boil. Add beans and sea salt and submerge kombu. Reduce heat and simmer covered until beans are tender. Remove from heat, drain, and serve or add to recipe as instructed.

Locally Grown

With so many government subsidies going to big farms and skipping over small organic local farms, all too often the very food we need and benefit from the most (organic, locally grown produce) is also the most expensive.

Even with the most beautiful produce, what you see is not always all that you get. The only way to truly know what is on your table is to know where it comes from—the seed, the soil, the plants, the farmer and the process it went through to get to your table. Knowing the source of your food does not require growing it or picking it yourself, but it does require taking an active role in gaining knowledge and finding resources.

SECURING CLEAN FOOD

Access to affordable clean food and fresh produce can vary dramatically depending on where you live. Here are some tips to help you be successful.

Ask your grocer. There's no need to turn your life and shopping routine upside down. Start by improving the offerings, wherever you shop, by simply asking for clean food. The more you ask, the more demand you create and the sooner you'll see local produce and cleaner packaged foods on your grocery store shelves. Do your research and ask for specific brands that are known to be clean.

Identify local farms. Learn what your local farms grow and produce. If you don't know of any, contact the Chamber of Commerce or search online by zip code on websites such as American Farmland Trust or Local Harvest (these websites and others are listed under *A Few of My Favorite Things, page 275*).

Get to know your farmer. Not all farmers take the same approach. Taking a farm tour, talking with the farmer and volunteering will empower you to make educated, healthy choices and give you the added benefits of greater appreciation and access to locally grown produce.

Join a CSA (Community Supported Agriculture). Purchasing a "share" provides the farmer with much needed capital before the growing season, when farm expenses are high, in exchange for a weekly share of produce throughout the harvest. Every CSA offers different benefits—opportunities to pick your own produce, buy other foodstuffs, pickup on a flexible schedule (some even have separate locations for pickup, saving you a trip to the farm), and of course, price. Shop around to find the CSA that works best for you.

Locate Farmers Markets. There is nothing like a farmers market for sourcing positive energy, an incredible sense of community, access to farmers and, oh yes, locally grown clean food. The same websites used to identify local farms can help you locate farmers markets, too.

Find buying clubs and coops. Clubs and coops can be found just about anywhere and come in many forms, ranging from grocery stores that offer memberships and discounts, to organized groups who order together from a variety of providers and distributors.

Grow Your Own. It doesn't get more locally grown than seeds that you raise in a container on a windowsill, a front porch, a rooftop or in a community garden, and you'll gain much more than a basket full of produce from the experience.

CLEAN FOOD ANIMAL PRODUCTS

My focus has always been to empower people to nourish themselves with fresh produce, whole grains, legumes, nuts, seeds and super-nutritional foods, including miso and sea vegetables. These are the foods we all need more of, no matter what else is on your plate. But clean also applies to other foods, such as animal products.

The reasons to include or exclude animal products from our diet are many and varied. Whatever your choice, it's important that these foods are clean, too. All of the tips previously mentioned for securing clean food also apply to animal products.

When shopping for produce, we look to reduce or eliminate exposure to pesticides and herbicides that are applied to the seed, the soil and the plant. We are increasingly aware of the nutrient density of produce and are empowered to make healthy choices as a result. When it comes to animal products, there are even more considerations.

If you choose to include animal products in your diet, it's important to consider their diet and environment. Raising animals in confined quarters, feeding them foods that are unnatural to their species, and treating them with antibiotics, hormones and steroids are common practices in conventional animal farming. The result can be highly-compromised animal products that present a host of health concerns for consumers.

The healthiest practices yield the healthiest products. Grass-fed pasture-grazing cows, fish swimming in clean open water, and free-roaming chickens that are allowed to eat bugs, grasses and seeds produce the cleanest products and are cleaner for the environment.

If animal protein is part of your diet, talk to your butcher or fishmonger, or seek out a local farmer who can answer your questions to ensure that you are getting humanely raised, naturally healthy and nutritious animal products.

WHAT TO AVOID

Non-natural diets of corn, soy or any food not appropriate for the species.

Non-organic diets of foods treated with herbicides and pesticides.

Animals given antibiotics, growth hormones or steroids.

Products preserved with nitrites, nitrates or sulfites.

Products made with artificial sweeteners.

Products containing unnatural flavorings such as MSG and "natural flavors."

Products using emulsifiers such as propylene glycol.

Fish that are unsustainable, overfished or raised in poorly managed fisheries.

Larger fish that are higher up on the food chain and therefore have more concentrated levels of mercury and other toxins.

The decision to include animal products in your diet is a personal one that should take into consideration potential positive and negative effects on your health. For sustainable good health, for our environment and ourselves, the concept of clean food can be applied to everything on your plate, whether influenced by religious beliefs, cultural traditions, humanitarian values or simply taste.

Breakfast

Without breakfast, I can't be held accountable for what happens during the rest of the day! Everything might seem fine early on, but once I start to dive, look out. Breakfast determines my energy, mood, ability to focus and attitude for the rest of the day. Without it, lunch comes too late to pick up the slack, and by midday I could be facedown on my keyboard, or even worse, binge eating in hope of recharging.

With a clean food breakfast for fuel, anything is possible. I am balanced, focused and positive. Best of all, I am able to make mindful choices throughout the day, responding thoughtfully to life rather than reacting to stress.

Breakfast can be tricky for many reasons. For some, it's hard to even imagine eating first thing in the morning, and making a meal at an early hour is even harder to fathom. Deciding what to eat is another issue that is complicated by everything from cultural norms and marketing to our own childhood memories of breakfast. Judgments about what constitutes breakfast food and what we "should" eat can prevent us from figuring out the foods that will provide the best start to the day.

Journaling is a powerful tool that can help you draw connections between diet and energy, behaviors and emotional responses. Keep track of what you eat, the time of day you ate it and how it makes you feel. It can take very little time to start seeing correlations between your diet and your health. I am almost always surprised when I look at my habits on paper. I am much more concious of the choices I make throughout the day when I know that I have to record every nibble and snack. Nothing makes me more accountable to myself than writing it down.

I like to think of my body as a car and food as my fuel (I use a toy windup car to illustrate this concept when I teach). Winding up the car is like eating a meal. When you let go, the car drives until the rubber band is out of stored energy. When I run out of fuel, I, too, struggle to "drive." There's one important difference. When I'm not fueled, my body pulls from my reserves. I can still "drive," but I become even more depleted, making a crash almost inevitable.

BREAKFAST IDEAS

The goal of fueling the day ahead makes the nutritional requirements for breakfast greater than any other meal. The elements that constitute a proper breakfast are likely to be different for each person and may even vary from day to day, depending on your routine.

Leftovers

Last night's dinner or yesterday's soup are often what work best for my body. Whole grains, vegetables and leafy greens are most likely to be a winter option, and can be reconstituted and reheated in a skillet with just a little water and in just a few minutes. Top the finished dish with avocado for a nutrient-rich and satisfying meal.

Milk

If you grew up drinking milk, adding it to cereal or granola, or using it in baked goods, you may be at a loss if you choose to, or have to, eliminate it now. There are a number of alternatives that will make this feel like no sacrifice at all. Look for rice, almond and hemp milks, which are available in almost every grocery store, or skip the package and processing and make your own rich, creamy and nutritious almond milk instead.

Dessert for breakfast

Grocery store shelves overflow with processed cereals, energy bars and baked goods that may sound like they offer good nutrition, but if the ingredient list reads more like a formula than real food, you're likely better off without.

The baked goods in this book are made with high-protein, gluten-free flours and natural sweeteners, so you can enjoy them without guilt any time of day. I depend on recipes like NoNo Bars *(page 272)* and Coconut Cacao Energy Bars *(page 143)* for protein-rich breakfast and snack options. I also use these recipes as templates, creating a variety of options by substituting different nuts, seeds, dried fruits and sweeteners. And when my family wants baked goods, I turn to one of my many dessert recipes. I feel much better about serving a Blondie *(page 205)* made with cannellini beans or even Carrot Cake *(page 80)* for breakfast than almost any processed and packaged alternative. And I often go as far as making a double batch of "dessert" just to make sure there's some leftover for breakfast the next day.

Smoothies

Smoothies appeal to my need for simplicity, not to mention my preferred cooking technique of dump and stir. Blended drinks that offer plant fiber (as opposed to extracted juices containing no fiber) fill me up and allow me to get a variety of nutrients all in one yummy glassful. While I've provided recipes on page 94, I highly recommend experimenting to discover your own favorite combinations. I load my blender with calcium-rich dark leafy greens, high-protein nuts and seeds, healthy fats from soaked chia seeds, flax or avocado, alkalinizing lemons and limes, high-antioxidant berries, green tea…. I'm running out of room, so I'll let you complete your own list!

HOMEMADE ALMOND MILK

1   cup raw almonds
2   cups water, plus extra for soaking
Optional: honey, maple syrup or maca root powder

Place almonds in bowl, cover well with water and soak 8 hours minimum or 36 hours max.

Drain almonds and rinse well. Place in blender and add 2 cups water. Blend on high until almonds are finely ground and water is white. Total blending time will depend on power of blender (4–6 minutes in conventional, 2–4 minutes in high-powered).

Drape cheesecloth over a large bowl and slowly pour blended almonds into bowl. Lift and gather sides of cheesecloth, twist to close and squeeze to press out milk. Taste milk and stir in sweetener of choice until desired sweetness is achieved. Store refrigerated in airtight container.

NOTE: Preheat oven or dehydrator to 120°F. Spread leftover almond meal evenly on a baking sheet or lined dehydrator shelf and dehydrate until dry (about 6 hours). Store in airtight container in freezer to use in recipes that call for almond meal.

MAKES 2 cups milk

NUTTY GRANOLA

4 cups rolled oats
1½ cups unsweetened coconut flakes
1 cup sliced almonds
1 cup chopped walnuts
1 cup pecans
1 cup sunflower seeds
1 tablespoon ground cinnamon
⅛ teaspoon ground cloves
½ cup melted virgin coconut oil
½ cup maple syrup
1 teaspoon almond extract

Preheat oven to 250°F.

In large bowl, mix together all dry ingredients. In separate bowl, whisk together oil, syrup and almond extract. Pour wet mixture over dry and stir to evenly coat. Transfer mixture to a 9 x 12-inch glass casseroles and bake 2 hours (until golden and dry). Turn off heat but leave granola in oven to cool and set completely before using a spatula to release granola and break into chunks. Store in airtight container.

MAKES 9½ cups

COCONUT ALMOND STEEL CUT OATS

1 cup steel cut oats
3½ cups water
¼ cup almond butter
¼ cup whole coconut milk
¼ teaspoon sea salt
1 teaspoon ground cinnamon
2 tablespoons maple syrup
Unsweetened coconut flakes, toasted
Sliced almonds, toasted

Place oats in pot with water and soak overnight. In the morning, turn heat to high and bring to boil. Reduce heat and simmer until creamy (20-25 minutes). Remove from heat and stir in almond butter, coconut milk, sea salt, cinnamon and maple syrup. Top each serving with coconut and sliced almonds as desired.

SERVES 6

Cereal

For years I assumed my family preferred sweets for breakfast and depended largely on oatmeal topped with maple syrup and fruit. When my girls started cooking for themselves years later, I was shocked to see them dress their oatmeal with just olive oil and sea salt. That's when I started thinking outside the box about breakfast.

"Cereal" doesn't mean it has to be processed and come in a box. In fact, almost any grain or combination of grains can be used to make a sweet or savory hot cereal that will warm and satisfy. Leftover cooked grains are perhaps the quickest and easiest place to start. Simply reconstitute and reheat grains in a small pan with water, juice, coconut water, your preferred milk alternative or even roasted vegetables and stock. Then finish it off with a variety of toppings, from maple syrup to toasted nuts or seeds, fresh fruit or berries, dried fruit, of course, olive oil and sea salt…or really spice it up with Cacao Chile Gomasio *(page 224)*!

My family still consumes more rolled oats than any other grain. When it's cold outside, we start the day with warm and creamy oatmeal or chewy and satisfying steel cut oats. To reduce cooking time, I soak them in water overnight. When I wake up in the morning, the rolled oats take just a couple of minutes to cook and the steel cut oats take just enough time for me to shower and dress. We make fruit crisps year round with in-season fruits and berries and enjoy them for breakfast, lunch, dinner and snacks. And rarely does a week go by that my home isn't filled with the aroma of freshly-baked granola.

Some of these favorite recipes are shared here, but it's a misnomer to call them breakfast foods, as we are just as likely to eat last night's lasagna for breakfast and homemade granola for dinner. When we do break free from convention, we are equally satisfied with these recipes, whether they are eaten for breakfast, lunch or dinner.

Pancakes

I'm convinced that my children measure my love by how often I make them pancakes. As a result, I make them often. Homemade pancakes are truly just as easy to prepare as the commercial mixes. My mom always grated apples into her pancakes to make them light and fluffy, so I do the same. My recipe for buckwheat pancakes is easy to double, in case your children gobble these up like mine do!

Chia Pudding

Chia seeds are a great source of omega 3 fats, but retain a tremendous amount of fluid. I soak seeds before eating or adding them to recipes to make them much easier to digest. This pudding is always in my refrigerator. I eat it straight out of the container, stir it into cooked grains and use it to add creamy goodness to smoothies. You can sweeten it to taste, but I find it satisfying without any sweetener at all. Once you master the basic pudding, you can go crazy adding nut and seed butters, fresh fruit, raw cacao or any number of other toppings.

The most important thing about breakfast is that we eat it. The breakfast ideas in this book represent just a fraction of the possibilities to be discovered when we let go of our preconceived notions and judgments about what breakfast foods "should" be and embrace what true nourishment "can" be. Hopefully they will inspire your own breakfast-making adventure. Even if you change nothing about the foods you eat for breakfast, you will benefit greatly from indulging in healthy breakfast habits — taking time to sit down, eating slowly, chewing thoroughly and allowing your body to assimilate the nutrients it needs. Let your first meal each day help you to negotiate life with energy, focus and good health.

BUCKWHEAT PANCAKES

½   cup buckwheat flour
⅔   cup white rice flour
1   teaspoon baking powder
1   cup almond or rice milk
½   cup peeled and grated apple, applesauce
    or mashed banana
¼   cup maple syrup, plus more for serving
1   tablespoon melted virgin coconut oil,
    plus extra for greasing griddle
1   teaspoon vanilla extract
Ground cinnamon
Garnish of seasonal fruit or berries

In medium bowl, whisk together buckwheat flour, rice flour and baking powder. In separate bowl, whisk together milk, apple or banana, maple syrup, coconut oil and vanilla. Pour wet ingredients into dry and fold to combine.
   Heat griddle over high heat and grease with coconut oil. Scoop batter by the ⅛ cupful and pour onto skillet. Cook until edges and top look almost dry. Flip pancakes and cook 1 minute longer. Remove from griddle and repeat until batter is used up, greasing griddle as needed. Serve with a drizzle of maple syrup, a dash of cinnamon and seasonal fruit or berries.

SERVES 4 (about 12 pancakes)

BASIC CHIA PUDDING

½   cup whole coconut milk
½   cup almond milk or coconut water
1   teaspoon vanilla extract
3   tablespoons chia seeds
Maple syrup
Ground cinnamon

In sealable glass bowl, whisk together coconut milk, almond milk and vanilla extract until consistency is smooth. Whisk in chia seeds, cover and refrigerate 2 hours (until mixture is thick, like pudding). When ready to eat, spoon into bowl and top with syrup and cinnamon as desired.

NOTE: For a smoother finished product, purée pudding with handheld blender before refrigerating.

SERVES 4

Shortcuts

Who doesn't need a shortcut every now and then? There are good reasons why grocery shelves are packed with quick and easy options for breakfast, lunch and dinner. We asked for convenience and we've paid the price. I strive to make whole meals, use fresh ingredients and keep a "clean" kitchen, but there's a time and place for many things, including packaged foods.

SELECTING THE BEST PACKAGED FOODS

If we're going to accept processed and packaged foods into our lives, we should be armed with the knowledge to separate the good from the bad.

Do I need it?

If you're looking at packaged food in the first place, you are already removed from the source and are compromising potential nutritional value. Before you take anything off the shelf, ask yourself if you could purchase it without the package. If it's something you've never prepared before, a package can actually be helpful. For instance, if you've never made whole grains before, the box or pouch often includes basic cooking instructions, a recipe and even a seasoning packet. Packaged grains are usually more expensive than those bought in bulk, plus there's the added waste of the package (which nobody needs). Try it once and move on from there.

TIPS FOR BUYING PACKAGED INGREDIENTS
Manufacturers may use different ingredients, some clean and some not so clean, to yield similar products. I've shared my favorite brands and resources in *A Few of My Favorite Things (page 275)*, but it's always best to read labels.

BEANS, CANNED FOODS
Look for brands that line their cans with BPA-free resin to avoid toxicity transfer to foods from endocrine-disrupting bisphenol-A.

EXTRA VIRGIN OLIVE OIL, VIRGIN COCONUT OIL
Look for cold pressed and unrefined.

MIRIN
Avoid brands that add corn syrup or artificial sweeteners. This sweet wine is naturally fermented, using water, rice, sea salt and koji (a natural fungus used to ferment).

MISO
There are many varieties, some with gluten (barley) and others without gluten (brown rice, chickpea…). Look for miso sold in glass containers or transfer it to glass when you get home, as fermented foods tend to pull toxins from plastic.

SPICES
Conventional brands often include wheat (gluten) to prevent caking. Know your source.

TAMARI, LIQUID AMINOS
Traditionally, these are non-wheat soy sauces, but some brands do contain wheat. Read labels every time, and for a soy-free alternative, look for raw coconut aminos.

TOFU
Look for brands that use natural coagulating agents like nigari (magnesium chloride derived from sea water or brine) instead of calcium sulfate (formulated in a laboratory), and go with organic or labeled as Non-GMO Project Verified.

VEGAN MAYONNAISE
Most varieties contain soy. Look for organic or Non-GMO Verified products or go with soy-free, grapeseed oil mayonnaise.

Canned beans are one of my time-saving vices. There is nothing like freshly made beans (especially chickpeas!), but when you haven't planned in advance or just don't have the time, having canned beans in the pantry can make a variety of recipes possible.

What's in it?

Skip over the marketing statements on the label and go straight to the ingredient list. If you can recognize how each item grows, you're doing well. If there are ingredients that sound more like formulas than food, put the package back and look for a different product. If you can't imagine how they grow, there's no guarantee your body will know what to do with them either.

Fresh or frozen?

I start every shopping trip in the produce section or at the farm, but the freezer section is also a regular stop. Organic frozen fruits and vegetables retain much of their original nutritional value, are cost effective and are great for smoothies, quick and easy frozen desserts, and many other uses. When my daughter was following a restricted rotation diet, she would eat frozen peas straight out of the bag for dessert. They couldn't replace cake or cookies, but they are indeed sweet.

Fast Food

I like to spend less than 30 minutes preparing meals and have created my recipes with that in mind. Sometimes, however, following a recipe just isn't in the cards or even necessary. An entire meal can be put together from just a few basic foods that require minimal preparation—cooked grains, greens, beans or tempeh, and squash or carrots. Top it all with a sprinkle of gomasio (sea salt and sesame seed condiment, *page 224)* or crumbled nori and you have a clean feast. These are ingredients that are almost always on hand in a clean food kitchen, so you always have the security of a wholesome balanced meal at your fingertips. This is a great way to upcycle leftovers and a great foundation from which to build a variety of different meals.

If you're reading this book, you're well on your way to creating healthy clean food meals. If a shortcut here or there can help you to prepare clean food recipes that feature a variety of fresh produce, than go for it. In the end, the goal is not only to nourish yourself with delicious clean food, but to achieve balance and wellness in all aspects of life. If you have a shortcut that can help you reach that goal, you're doing alright!

Fill your plate with foods that nourish you;
bless all of your choices, even if they serve something
other than your best nutritional needs; listen to your body;
and be gentle on yourself.
Do the best you can, make one choice at a time,
and enjoy every bite.

SPRING
A FRESH BEGINNING

I balance on the edge of winter and spring, with breezes cool and gentle, trees bare and still, spring's arrival greatly anticipated. Patches of crusty white snow reveal the ground that lies beneath. I look down and discover the first unopened cone of a purple crocus. In that moment, I leave winter behind and fill myself with thoughts for the season to come. Is there any season more welcome than spring? This is the season of birth, renewal and hope. It starts with longer days and warmer temperatures—tempting and teasing us to shed the layers that protected us through winter. There is a constant buzz outside my window, as if everyone and everything has awakened. The sun's rays slowly open each blossom and each door, but cold and rain come just as often forcing those same doors shut. The rhythms and moods of spring can be ever changing, but warmer days and increasing sunshine lure me out regardless. Wild foraged foods like ramps and fiddleheads give this season tastes like none other. I fill my plate with tender sweet peas and fava beans, baby artichoke hearts and asparagus, and I feel lighter as a result—mind, body and soul. In the end, this season of greatest change, that starts with barely a glimpse of life, will bloom in a rainbow of color, reflecting the nourishment I've missed all winter long.

CONTENTS

Spring Cleaning

Toxins are everywhere—in our food, our water and the air we breathe. A little internal cleaning can provide a welcome sense of renewal and improved health, and no time of year lends itself more to cleansing than spring.

After winter's heavy and warming foods and food preparations, Mother Nature gives us exactly what we need in spring. Tender baby greens, sprouts and bitter herbs are designed to naturally detoxify, support and regenerate our digestive system. Following her lead, we can safely cleanse without feeling starved or deprived.

While cleansing can lighten us emotionally and physically, it is not a weight loss program. Bouncing between extremes can create stress and imbalance. Start slowly, laying a foundation and developing habits that support long-term health.

Clearing away clutter on the inside can lend itself to clearer thinking and a deeper connection to the body. This is a great opportunity to learn which foods and food preparations work for your unique constitution and which don't. Cleansing can also help us move through emotional issues, break harmful habits, gain mental clarity and reconnect spiritually.

The reasons to cleanse are ones that only you can determine, and the method will be the one that nourishes you in a gentle way, uses the resources you have available, and leaves you in a stronger and healthier place—body, mind and soul.

CLEANSING FOODS

Eating clean year-round allows us to nourish our bodies, reduce inflammation and acidity, build digestive strength and healthy intestinal flora, and maintain optimal health. Under ideal circumstances, this makes the need for cleansing minimal. That said, pitfalls and slips are part of all of our lives, as are temptations, indulgences and stresses that make gentle cleansing a worthwhile effort to get back on track and feeling well.

Just as eating clean will look different for each person, so will cleansing. For one, giving up artificial ingredients could be powerful and healing, whereas the next person may want to give up packaged processed foods altogether, and a third person may focus on seasonal fresh produce and super-nutritionals.

Our motivations to cleanse may be different, but the foods and tools we look to for supporting our goals are often the same. Remember, just eating clean can be all the cleanse you need. That said, there are specific foods and practices that can be strong allies, especially when incorporated into a clean food diet. Many of them are featured regularly in my recipes, but calling them out empowers us to use them to achieve not only delicious meals, but good health as well.

Like eating clean, cleansing allows us to reduce inflammation created from processed foods, artificial ingredients, preservatives, conventional animal protein, carbohydrates, sugar, caffeine, stress and lack of sleep. This is a time when hydration is key, as is bringing in more fiber (to flush toxins) and supporting gut health with probiotics (preferably from raw and fermented foods). Simply bringing in one new clean food a week is always a safe place to start. For more powerful cleansing, consider reducing or eliminating inflammatory foods such as sugar, caffeine and artificial ingredients. Replace those with the cleansing foods listed on the following page, and always consult with a physician before considering a more extreme cleanse.

GREENS AND CRUCIFEROUS VEGETABLES:

Rich with alkalinizing minerals and detoxifying sulfur and chlorophyll.
Kale, broccoli, cauliflower, watercress, mustard greens, arugula, cabbage… (I could make this list go on for days!). Many of these we eat all winter, even all year, long. For more powerful cleansing, shift from steamed, sautéed or roasted preparations to raw, juiced or sprouted.

DANDELION LEAVES AND ROOTS:

For liver and digestive support, anti-inflammatory properties, antimicrobial, cholesterol-lowering and a rich source of antioxidants, vitamins and minerals.
Dandelion greens can be added to salad mixes, tossed with other dark leafy greens and stirred into healing soups and broths (like miso). If still too bitter, start with dandelion tea (made from both the leaves and roots and available at most natural food stores), or blanch leaves in hot water for 30–60 seconds and then drain before adding to your recipe.

LEMON:

For increasing alkalinity to counter our highly acid-forming diets and lifestyles.
Add to room-temperature or warm water. Use as an alternative to vinegar, add to smoothies and juices (skin and all), and squeeze over greens, grains, vegetables and legumes.

GARLIC, ONIONS AND TURMERIC:

For antiviral, antibacterial, anti-inflammatory, antiseptic, antibiotic and detoxification properties.
Use liberally, both raw and cooked. Allow garlic to sit briefly after mincing and before use to allow the anticancer, antimicrobial, lipid-lowering, antioxidant properties of the compound allicin to develop.

SEA VEGETABLES:

For chlorophyll and minerals that detoxify and balance pH.
Arame, wakame and dulse will need to be reconstituted in warm water and drained before being added to soups, salads or grains. Sheet nori does not need to be reconstituted and can be used plain or toasted for wraps and rolls, shredded for toppings or eaten on its own. Kombu can be added to cooking grains and legumes to infuse them with minerals and reduce their gaseous properties. Kelp, most often found powdered, can be sprinkled on a variety of dishes and easily added to smoothies and dressing.

SUPER GREENS:

For adding chlorophyll and flushing toxins.
Spirulina, chlorella and wheatgrass are most commonly found as supplements or powdered so they can be added to smoothies and juices.

MILK THISTLE SEED:

For regenerating the liver.
Whole seeds can be ground and added to whole-grain dishes such as oatmeal and granola (my favorites), smoothies or baked goods. Milk thistle is also available in teabags and as a tincture or supplement.

NETTLES:

For anti-inflammatory properties and deep immune support.
Fresh nettles can be added to teas, soups and stocks, salads, pestos…. Dried nettles can be used for making your own teas and seasoning blends and packaged nettle tea is also readily available at natural food stores.

RAW LOCAL HONEY:

For immune and digestive support, minerals, antioxidants, antiviral, antibacterial and antifungal properties.
Raw local honey can be used topically to heal wounds, burns and irritations. It can be taken orally to counter environmental allergies and boost the immune system, and can be added to drinks, dressings and baked goods as a natural sweetener if desired.

CLEANSING PRACTICES

Cleansing is as much about listening to your body and developing healthy habits as it is about detoxifying. Imbalance, inflammation and disease can be caused by a host of lifestyle and dietary choices. Making time for these practices helps in all seasonal transitions, minimizes the negative impact of stress and gives us the strength to make healthy choices day in and day out. Spring is the perfect time to restart any practices we've let slip over the winter months.

Sleep: A poor night's sleep and my stomach aches, my focus is compromised, my energy wanes, my temper shortens and my ability to make healthy choices is challenged. Perhaps worst of all, I run on adrenaline, overproducing cortisol and setting myself up for a variety of health problems from thyroid imbalance to depression, digestive issues and much more. Over the long term, inadequate sleep weakens the immune system, contributes to inflammation, negatively affects brain function and is even linked to obesity. Splurge on sleep for just two weeks, and you are likely to see positive changes in your mental and physical health.

Mindfulness: Mindfulness comes in many forms, from meditation and yoga to prayer, walking and even eating. Practice connecting with your breath, letting go of tension in every muscle, and being aware of the moment. Start by breathing in positive intentions and exhaling physical and emotional stress. The more we practice going to this place of calm, the more skilled we become at calling upon it later when we are stressed or faced with temptation, and the more we benefit from the healing stillness of meditation.

A mindfulness practice around eating can be a powerful way to heal relationships with food. Before eating, give thanks. Honor the food and acknowledge those with whom you get to share it. Note what it is, where it came from, the farmer, the soil, the seed. Engage your senses by looking at it, smelling the aromas and, yes, even tasting it modestly before eating. Appreciate the subtlety of flavors, textures and tastes and savor each bite. Remember, digestion starts in your mouth with the enzymes secreted there, so slowing down and chewing thoroughly will improve your digestion and give you more nutrition from less food. Eat with love, compassion and the intention of being healed, and you will give those very properties to the foods on your plate.

Journal: Journaling is one of the more powerful methods I know of to listen to your body and figure out which foods and practices are working for you and which are not. Create a chart with three columns: one to record the foods you eat and your activities, one for the time of day and one to note how your feel (energy level, mood, ability to focus, sleep patterns…). In just days, you will start to see correlations between what you eat and how you respond physically, mentally and emotionally. It's always an interesting study to see the difference between what I think I eat and what I actually consume. Just a few days of journaling is often the accountability I need to get back on track.

Exercise: Spring is a perfect time to get outdoors. Movement means better digestion and extra sunlight means more essential vitamin D to help absorb nutrients from your food. Find a routine that works for you and get your heart rate up for 30 minutes a day. This is a great way to cleanse without changing your diet at all!

Stretch: Stretching releases the physical and mental tension caused by stress, and can have similar benefits as your mindfulness practice. If you don't know where to begin, enroll in a gentle yoga class or find a video online. Stretching increases flexibility, brings blood to the muscles and supports proper alignment, which in turn, supports almost all bodily functions.

Hydrate: Hydration is key to metabolism, blood pressure, digestion and many other systems, and yet sometimes it can be a struggle. When water just doesn't cut it, it helps to have some other tools in your arsenal. A wedge of alkalinizing lemon is a healthy and tasty way to dress up a glass of water.

Whether you're on a well or have city water, what comes out of your tap is likely cleaner and greener than drinking water packaged in plastic. Regular testing can help you determine exactly what's in your drinking and bathing water. A variety of filters are available to help reduce

the amount of pesticides, herbicides, chemicals, detergents and excessive minerals and fluoride commonly found in municipal water.

Teas such as green tea, white tea and herbal blends are other options that provide not only hydration but also powerful medicine. See page 219 for information about experimenting with blending teas and herbs to suit your taste and health goals. Simply bring water to just under a boil, remove from heat, stir in herbs, steep, strain and drink hot or chilled.

Go Raw: Cooked foods sustain us through the colder months, but living raw foods are always important to include in the mix, delivering abundant nutrients that can otherwise break down when heated. Be sure to include beneficial lacto-fermented foods that significantly improve the presence of healthy gut bacteria and support the immune system.

Neti Pot: I often forget about the neti pot until I'm completely stuffed up, at which point one of my daughters will inevitably say, "Mom, why aren't you using the neti pot?" One cup of room temperature water, 5 drops of goldenseal tincture, ¼ teaspoon sea salt and ¼ teaspoon baking soda mixed together and used with the neti pot as a sinus flush can make all the difference when it comes to managing spring allergies.

The question is not if cleansing in spring is prudent, but rather what approach is best suited for you. Whether you focus simply on bringing in more raw vegetables or creating a program utilizing a variety of cleansing foods, tonics and practices, make it realistic and achievable. "Now" is always a great time to start eating clean and living well. Practicing these health-supporting habits is the best way to make them permanent.

Cleaning Up Your Home and Environment

Once I have addressed my physical needs, my focus turns outward. Clearing away clutter in the home can be liberating, improve mental clarity, relieve stress, improve energy, improve productivity and set us up for healthier living moving forward.

DECLUTTER

Projects in the home can feel endless, but taking on just one at a time can help us to feel organized and even more motivated for the next project. I start with the spaces I use the most—the pantry, my closet and my office—and here's how I do it:

1. Pick one space to declutter – a room, a drawer, a closet…

2. Pull out everything – all the spices in the pantry, all the sweaters in the closet or all of the piles on the desk.

3. Clean the space – this might be a good time to try the homemade cleaning products on the next page.

4. Sort all items – into categories to keep, sell, donate, recycle and trash.

5. Clean and organize – fold clothes, file papers, shred unimportant documents, dispose of old herbs and spices….

6. Return items to keep – and pack up items to sell, donate and recycle.

7. Make a plan – once your space is clean and organized, create a plan for the items to be repurposed.

8. Breathe.

I don't know about you, but I feel better already!

CLEAN CLEANERS

Cleaning indoors can reduce allergies, kill germs, improve sleep and reduce mental and physical stress, as long as it's done in a clean way. Many commercial cleaning products can fill your home with toxic chemicals, fumes and dyes connected to serious health concerns, from allergies and asthma to reproductive disorders and cancer. Learn if your products contain toxic ingredients by visiting the Environmental Working Group online at EWG.org.

Homemade cleaning products are easy to make, inexpensive and every bit as effective. Here are some of my favorites:

Baking Soda: I grew up with a box of baking soda in the back of the refrigerator as a deodorizer, but today I also use it on a damp sponge to remove marks from painted walls and as a nonscratching cleaner for metal and stained surfaces. Combined with white vinegar or lemon juice, baking soda foams, making cleaning even faster and more effective. Baking soda will even unclog drains if you pour it down the drain followed by vinegar, let it sit and foam for 20 minutes and then flush it with water.

Borax: Disinfecting, bleaching and deodorizing, borax is great for tough stains, grout, tile and making your own laundry detergent. Be careful not to get it on your skin as it can be irritating.

Castile Soap: I use olive oil–based castile soap regularly as an all-purpose cleaner and soap for hands, body and even the dog.

Coconut Oil: There are countless uses for coconut oil besides cooking. I use it to season pots and pans, condition wooden cutting boards, and as a moisturizer and conditioner for skin and hair.

Distilled White Vinegar: Distilled white vinegar disinfects and cuts through dirt. Add ¼ cup vinegar to a gallon of water to clean wooden floors. Add 2 tablespoons baking soda to make an all-purpose cleaner for tubs, sinks and chrome fixtures. To mask the vinegar smell, add 5–10 drops of essential oils.

Essential Oils: Lemon, cinnamon and peppermint are among the therapeutic grade essential oils I add to my cleaning products for aroma and antibacterial properties. For a powerhouse cleaner, try Thieves Essential Oil Blend.

Felted Wool Balls: Throw felted wool balls into your dryer and let the lanolin act as a natural fabric softener. They'll also decrease the amount of time and energy required to dry your clothing. Available in health-food stores and online, these can last up to a year (depending on how many loads of laundry you do). Of course, hanging clothes to dry saves even more energy and leaves clothes feeling soft and smelling fresher than even the best "fresh air" scented fabric softener.

Lemon Juice: As good for cleaning your home as it is for cleaning and alkalinizing your body, lemon juice cuts through grease especially well and can be used undiluted directly on mold and mildew.

Microfiber Cloths: I remove dust from my entire home with just a few microfiber cloths and no product at all. Wash, hang to dry and reuse. Now *that* is clean!

Sunlight: If only we could bottle it! Sunlight is strong medicine for fighting mold and bacteria and keeping your home environment clean and healthy. Open the blinds, let the sunshine in, and while you're at it, open the windows to move the old air out and the fresh air in.

Thieves: Perhaps the most powerful of all of the natural cleaning products, Thieves is a blend of therapeutic essential oils with strong antibacterial, antimicrobial, antiseptic and antiviral properties. Thieves can help support a healthy body and a healthy environment. It can be taken internally, used topically, on surfaces in your home and even diffused into the air. Each application will require a different recipe. I've highlighted some of my standbys below. It's important when making Thieves—or when using any essential oils—to purchase high-quality "therapeutic grade" oils.

THIEVES ESSENTIAL OIL BLEND

1 tablespoon therapeutic grade clove essential oil
1 tablespoon therapeutic grade lemon essential oil
1 tablespoon therapeutic grade cinnamon bark essential oil
1 teaspoon therapeutic grade eucalyptus essential oil
1 teaspoon therapeutic grade rosemary essential oil

Combine all ingredients in a dark apothecary bottle that has a top with a dropper. Seal, shake and store out of direct sunlight. Shake again before using.

ALL-PURPOSE CLEANER
16 drops Thieves
1 quart water

Combine Thieves and water in spray bottle. Close bottle, shake well, spray surfaces and wipe with clean cloth.

HEALING RUB
1 drop Thieves
4 drops organic virgin coconut oil or organic extra virgin olive oil

Blend Thieves with oil and rub into bottoms of feet or use to massage shoulders or neck.

IMMUNE SUPPORT
1 drop Thieves
1 cup water, tea or juice

Add Thieves to water, tea or juice, stir and drink.

AIR FRESHENER
10 drops Thieves
1 cup water

Combine Thieves and water in dark spray bottle, seal and shake. Shake again before using.

Moving Outside

At last, it's time to turn our attention outside to the many activities that support our efforts to eat clean and live well. While clean food is the common thread, there is another underlying link that makes each of these activities even more powerful than they already are. Whether working in my garden, turning my compost, or just sitting on the front stoop, each spring I am greeted by friends and neighbors doing the same, and I am convinced that that connection does almost as much for my health and wellbeing as any clean food can. Add one or a few of these activities, and you will make a difference not only to your own health, but may inspire others as well.

Planting Seeds: Do yourself a favor and plant at least one seed, and if you have children, have them plant seeds too. A small backyard garden, community garden, or pots for your porch or windowsill will allow you to better understand and appreciate the foods that sustain us. Planting just a few herbs that make it into your summer salads may inspire you to become a farmer, or may convince you that growing is not your thing and lead you to find a local farmer to support. Perhaps caring for your plants will become part of your mindfulness practice. No matter what, you will be well served by the knowledge of what it takes to grow food, and that holds true for children as well. The more educated they are about their food, from growing to cooking to serving, the more open they will be to try a variety of foods and make healthy choices that sustain their own good health.

Composting: Separating food and garden waste from trash can dramatically reduce the amount of garbage you produce, and with a little bit of effort can yield nutrient-rich compost to nourish your soil and any plants you are growing.

The separating is easy, it's the composting that can be intimidating, but there are options. Even if you don't have space to compost, you can purchase a container for storing scraps and donate them regularly to a farm, an individual or a business that composts. Find a place where you can drop it off, or arrange with a service that will pick it up (more and more of these services are becoming available every day).

If you'd like to try composting, all it takes is a little bit of effort, temperatures above 50°F, moisture and a healthy balance of green and dry matter. Composting can be done in a purchased container or in homemade bins, and everything from yard clippings and leaves to trimmings from produce can be composted.

Between composting and purchasing less packaged food, you'll be shocked by how much you can reduce the amount of garbage you produce. Composting is forgiving, too. I throw my scraps into my compost pile straight through the winter, amending the pile with dry matter come spring, and achieving rich and beautiful compost to spread on my garden all summer long.

Conserving water: As water becomes more scarce, conservation becomes more crucial. Measures like using rain barrels to collect rain water for watering indoor and outdoor plants and gardens are well worthwhile to reduce consumption of this valuable natural resource. As important are any efforts to use water more efficiently.

Community Supported Agriculture (CSA) and Farmers Markets

Before we get cooking, there's one more spring activity worth making a priority—locating resources for locally grown produce. CSAs allow you to buy a share of a farm's yield for the growing season while providing essential working capital that allows a farmer to pay the significant upfront costs of farming. In return, you receive a weekly share of produce during the harvest season. Everyone wins with a CSA, but they can sell out quickly, so don't put this off until summer.

Early spring is the best time to seek out and join a CSA and learn about the farmers markets in your area. Online resources like the USDA and LocalHarvest.org allow you to search by zip code to find resources near you, but no internet search can take the place of connecting with friends and community members to learn from their experiences.

If you're new to joining a CSA, doing so with a friend is a great way to share the adventure (and work)! If you're not used to getting a basket of fresh produce each week, your CSA experience may be overwhelming. Splitting a share will allow you to ease into it and see what it's all about. You'll definitely appreciate having someone in the same shoes to bounce ideas off of when you find yourself home staring at a basket of produce waiting to be prepared or stored.

While a CSA will introduce you to one farm, farmers markets will allow you to meet many farmers and producers, are a fun way to connect to the community, and often feature local goods, musicians, artisans, service organizations and even cookbook authors.

Best of all, any effort to find and eat locally grown foods will reward you with quality fresh produce that will keep you in balance with your environment, and will connect you with others who share the same values and journey.

WHERE TO BEGIN

Little can motivate us to get outside and get active more than being inside all winter long,
but spring can be overwhelming with so much to do and the desire to lighten up, get outside and be active.
What's most important is not that we do it all, but that we know what the opportunities are
and become empowered to do those things that speak to us that enhance our health and our lives.
Even small actions can lead us toward better health for our environment and ourselves.

Wild Ramp Pesto

EVERY SEASON SHOULD HAVE AT LEAST ONE PESTO. Enjoy this one while you can, because ramps don't stick around for long. Use it as a spread for sandwiches or grilled bread, as a sauce for tossing with pasta, or as a savory condiment stirred into hot or cold soups (like Spring Minestrone with Baby Artichokes, *page 47*).

1 cup chopped ramps (wild leeks), bulbs and leaves

¼ cup coarsely chopped fresh flat-leaf parsley

¼ cup toasted pine nuts

¼ cup cashews

¼ cup extra virgin olive oil

3 tablespoons lemon juice

½ teaspoon sea salt

In food processor, combine ramps and parsley and process to mince. Add pine nuts and cashews and process to combine. With processor running, slowly pour in olive oil and lemon juice. Turn processor off, scrape down sides, add sea salt and process until all ingredients are well combined and smooth. Season to taste with salt and process one final time. Remove from processor and serve, or refrigerate or freeze in airtight container.

MAKES about 1½ cups

Artichoke Tapenade

I USE THIS DIP RELIGIOUSLY FOR SPRING ENTERTAINING. And since canned artichokes are available year round, I also use it any time of year as a filler for sandwiches and wraps (especially good with watercress and sliced tomatoes), as a spread on crackers or grilled bread, and even thinned with olive oil and tossed with pasta.

---

2   garlic cloves, peeled

6   sun-dried tomatoes

1½   cups artichoke hearts, drained

¾   cup pitted Cerignola olives

1   tablespoon capers

3   tablespoons extra virgin olive oil

2   tablespoon lemon juice

Salt and freshly ground pepper

Pinch of red pepper flakes

With food processor running, drop in garlic and sun-dried tomatoes to mince. Turn processor off and add artichoke hearts, olives and capers and pulse to chop and combine. Scrape down sides of container. Add olive oil, lemon juice, salt, ground pepper and pepper flakes and process to combine until somewhat smooth with flecks of individual ingredients visible. Serve or store refrigerated in airtight container.

MAKES about 1½ cups

Polenta Croutons

CRISPY ON THE OUTSIDE, soft and savory on the inside...these are much more than just your ordinary croutons. Baked or fried, you're going to love the texture and dimension these little bites of polenta add to your salad.

Extra virgin olive oil

3½ cups vegetable stock or water

¼ teaspoon sea salt

1 cup polenta

1 teaspoon dried parsley

Lightly oil rimmed baking sheet with olive oil and set aside.

In medium pot over medium-high heat, bring stock to boil. Add salt and, stirring continuously, slowly pour in polenta. Add parsley and stir until well combined. Reduce heat and simmer covered, stirring occasionally to prevent clumping, until polenta is creamy and thick (about 25 minutes). Remove from heat and pour into baking sheet. Evenly spread polenta to a ¾-inch thickness and refrigerate until firm (about 30 minutes).

Preheat oven to 400°F.

Remove polenta from refrigerator and cut into ¾-inch cubes. Separate cubes so not touching, place in oven and bake 15 minutes. Remove from oven, flip cubes and bake until dry and firm on the outside, about 15 minutes longer. Remove from oven and set aside to cool slightly before using.

Croutons can be made in advance, brought to room temperature and stored in an airtight container in the refrigerator or freezer. When ready to use, reheat in 350°F oven for 10 minutes.

MAKES about 3 cups

VARIATION
Instead of baking, pan-fry croutons in extra virgin olive oil for 3 minutes, pat with paper towel to absorb excess oil, and use.

Pretty In Pink Radishes

THERE ARE THREE REASONS TO FERMENT FOODS. The first is for healthy intestinal flora (see Love Your Belly Kraut, *page 165,* and Kimchi, *page 166)*. The second is to preserve the harvest. And the third is because they're delicious. This process varies slightly from those used to make sauerkraut and kimchi, and will work for most vegetables.

---

6   garlic cloves, thinly sliced

4   2-inch sprigs fresh dill

12   peppercorns

Pinch of red pepper flakes

3   bunches globe-type red radishes, such as cherry belle

2   small watermelon radishes

1   tablespoon plus 2 teaspoons sea salt

2   cups water

TOOLS

2   pint-size canning jars with lids

Weights (anything that will fit inside your jar to keep radishes submerged)

Cheesecloth and rubber bands

Divide garlic, dill, peppercorns and pepper flakes between canning jars. Wash radishes well, trim and discard roots and greens, and slice radishes into ¼-inch rounds. Pack firmly in jars so varieties are mixed and jars are two-thirds full.

In separate bowl, make brine by combining salt and water and stirring until salt is completely dissolved. Pour brine into canning jars until radishes are just covered (you may not need all of the brine). Leave space at the top of each jar to prevent brine from overflowing when you press radishes down below level of brine. Place weight in mouth of each canning jar to hold radishes down so they are fully submerged in brine. Cover with cheesecloth, secure with rubber bands and set aside to ferment.

Check radishes daily. Should brine evaporate and expose radishes, make more using the same salt to water ratio above. Any mold that appears can be skimmed off and discarded (this is possible if pieces are not fully submerged in brine). Radishes will be lightly pickled within 24 hours and will become more sour the longer they are left to ferment. When taste is as desired, cover and refrigerate to slow fermentation.

Note: I refrigerate my radishes after about 7–10 days of fermentation.

MAKES about 2 cups

Red Lentil Soup with Cumin and Spinach

THE SEEDS FROM LAST FALL'S SPINACH are often the first things to grow in my garden in the spring (beating out even the weeds). They offer an early taste of the season to come and give me all the motivation I need to get back into the garden after a long cold winter.

2 tablespoons extra virgin olive oil

1 medium red onion, chopped

2 garlic cloves, minced

2 celery stalks, chopped

2 carrots, sliced into thin rounds

1½ cups chopped tomatoes

1 cup red lentils, rinsed

5 cups vegetable stock or water

2 tablespoons red wine vinegar

1 teaspoon ground cumin

½ teaspoon paprika

¼ teaspoon sea salt

4 cups firmly packed spinach leaves

Freshly ground pepper

In large Dutch oven over medium heat, sauté onion and garlic in olive oil until soft (about 3 minutes). Add celery, carrots, tomatoes and lentils and stir to combine. Add vegetable stock, vinegar, cumin, paprika and sea salt and bring to boil. Reduce heat and simmer until lentils are soft (about 20 minutes).

Fold in spinach leaves and press to submerge so they wilt and cook. Simmer 2 minutes longer. Remove from heat, season to taste with pepper and serve.

SERVES 6

Fava Bean Soup with Sugar Snap Peas and Parsley Pesto

THE LURE OF FRESH FAVA BEANS at the farmstand is so strong I rarely walk away without them. While favas don't fit my preferred "dump and stir" cooking technique, they are surprisingly simple to prepare and worth the minimal effort.

PARSLEY PESTO

¼ cup cashews

¼ cup firmly packed fresh flat-leaf parsley

3 tablespoons extra virgin olive oil

1 tablespoon lemon juice

Pinch of sea salt

SOUP

2 pounds fava beans in pods (to yield 2 cups shelled)

2 bunches ramps (wild leeks)

2 tablespoons extra virgin olive oil

4 cups vegetable stock

2 cups sugar snap peas, strings removed, cut on an angle into ½-inch pieces

Sea salt and freshly ground pepper

¼ cup chopped fresh chives

2 tablespoons cold-pressed roasted pistachio oil

In a food processor, combine cashews and parsley and pulse to chop. Add olive oil, lemon juice and sea salt and pulse to combine. Scrape down sides of container, turn processor on and process until smooth. Set pesto aside.

Remove favas from pods by snapping the tips and pulling down to remove strings. Open pod, remove beans and discard pods. Bring 2 inches of water to boil in medium pot with steamer rack. Steam favas 1 minute, remove from heat, and rinse under cold water. Set aside for 5 minutes or until skins start to shrivel. Pinch skin at end to slit open and peel beans. Discard inedible peels and set favas aside.

Trim and discard root end from ramps, separate white bulbs from green leaves and chop both crosswise into ¼-inch pieces. In Dutch oven over medium heat, sauté white parts of ramps in olive oil until soft (about 3 minutes). Add stock and bring to simmer.

Add prepared favas and sugar snap peas to soup along with green parts of ramps and simmer to heat through. Scoop pesto into soup and stir to combine. Season to taste with salt and pepper and serve topped with chives and a drizzle of pistachio oil.

SERVES 4

Spring Onion and Quinoa Soup with Roasted Asparagus

THIS SOUP IS EVERYTHING I WANT FROM A SPRING MEAL. Its broth is infused with the sweetness of spring onions, and high-protein quinoa adds just enough body to satisfy. I roast the asparagus first and add it last so that it retains its taste and texture, adding another dimension to this soup that always hits the spot.

1	bunch asparagus
2	tablespoons extra virgin olive oil
¼	teaspoon coarse sea salt
3	medium spring onions
3	garlic cloves, thinly sliced
½	cup uncooked quinoa
6	cups vegetable stock
1	tablespoon mirin
Sea salt and freshly ground pepper	

Preheat oven to 400°F.

Bend asparagus near bottom of stalks to break off dried ends at natural breaking point. Discard ends and cut remaining stalks on an angle into 2-inch pieces. Drizzle with 1 tablespoon olive oil, sprinkle with coarse sea salt and spread on baking sheet. Roast 20 minutes or until asparagus is tender and lightly browned. Remove from oven and set aside.

Trim spring onions and slice white bulbs and light green stems into thin rounds (discard dark green stems). Drizzle remaining 1 tablespoon olive oil in Dutch oven over medium-high heat and add sliced onions and garlic. Sauté until onions start to soften (about 2 minutes). Rinse quinoa, add to mixture and toast 2 minutes to lightly toast. Add stock and mirin and bring to boil. Reduce heat and simmer covered until quinoa is tender (about 20 minutes). Season to taste with salt and pepper, keeping in mind that soup will get saltier from roasted asparagus. Top each serving with a scoopful of roasted asparagus and serve.

Note: Spring onions can be hard to find, not because they're not available, but because grocery stores tend to label them inconsistently. Look for slightly overgrown scallions with a rounder white bulb.

SERVES 4

Healing Mung Bean Soup

MUNG BEANS HAVE BEEN USED FOR CENTURIES to detoxify and heal. High in protein and rich in soluble fiber to lower cholesterol, this recipe is as much my spring cleansing tonic as it is a soothing and delicious one-pot meal.

1   tablespoon virgin coconut oil

1   onion, chopped

2   celery stalks, chopped

2   carrots, chopped

1   teaspoon ground turmeric

1   cup dried mung beans, rinsed

1½   cups chopped tomatoes

4   cups water or vegetable stock

2   bay leaves

¼   cup chopped fresh cilantro

1   tablespoon ume plum vinegar

Freshly ground pepper

Melt coconut oil in Dutch oven over medium heat. Add onion and sauté 3 minutes. Add celery, carrots and turmeric and sauté until just soft (about 3 minutes longer). Stir in mung beans, tomatoes and water or stock. Submerge bay leaves, increase heat to high and bring soup to boil. Reduce heat and simmer covered 45 minutes. Remove from heat and discard bay leaves. Stir in cilantro and ume plum vinegar, season to taste with pepper and serve.

SERVES 6

Spring Minestrone with Baby Artichokes

MUCH OF THE SEASONAL FRESH PRODUCE I purchase on Fridays at the farm goes straight from the bag to the pot. I add a can of chopped tomatoes and call it minestrone. Everyone is happy.

1   lemon, halved

5   baby artichokes

2   spring onions or
    1 small red onion

6   garlic cloves

2   tablespoons extra virgin
    olive oil

½   bulb fennel, cored and
    chopped

1   carrot, sliced into thin
    rounds

1½ cups cooked chickpeas

1½ cups chopped tomatoes

6   cups vegetable stock

¾   pound baby potatoes,
    cut into wedges

1   heaping tablespoon
    chopped fresh oregano
    (or 2 teaspoons dried)

1   bay leaf

1   cup shelled fresh peas

1   tablespoon balsamic
    vinegar

¼   cup chopped fresh
    flat-leaf parsley

Sea salt and freshly ground
    pepper

Fill a bowl with 6 cups cold water. Squeeze lemon into water and drop one lemon half into bowl. Working one artichoke at a time, slice off and discard top one-third. Immediately rub cut edge with remaining lemon half. Pull off tough outer leaves until you reach tender light green leaves (it may feel like you're peeling more than necessary, but darker leaves will remain tough). Peel stem, trim and discard end of stem and halve artichoke lengthwise. Cut each half into 3 wedges and place immediately in lemon water to keep from browning. Repeat with remaining artichokes and set aside.

Slice onion bulbs and light green stems into thin rounds (discard dark green parts) or peel and mince red onion. Mince 2 cloves of garlic.

Heat 1 tablespoon olive oil in Dutch oven over medium heat. Add onions and minced garlic and sauté 2 minutes. Add fennel and carrot and sauté 2 minutes longer. Add chickpeas, chopped tomatoes and vegetable stock and stir. Drain artichokes and add to soup along with potatoes and oregano. Submerge bay leaf and simmer until artichokes are cooked through (about 25 minutes).

Thinly slice remaining 4 garlic cloves. Heat remaining 1 tablespoon olive oil in small skillet over low heat. Place garlic slices in single layer and fry each side until golden brown. Remove from heat and transfer slices to paper towel. Stir garlic-infused oil into soup. Remove soup from heat and discard bay leaf. Stir in peas, vinegar and parsley. Season to taste with salt and pepper and serve topped with garlic chips.

Note: A rind of Parmigano-Reggiano cooked in with soup will infuse it with amazing flavor.

SERVES 6

Kohlrabi, Beet and Micro Greens Salad

GROWING MICRO GREENS IS A FUN INDOOR PROJECT that requires just a container with drainage, organic potting soil and a sunlit windowsill. Just in case you don't get to growing your own, these high-protein, vitamin-rich sprouted greens are easy to find in most grocery stores, too.

¾ cup peeled and julienned kohlrabi (purple or green)

¾ cup peeled and julienned golden beet

¾ cup peeled and julienned Chioggia beet

4 medium scallions, spring garlic or chives

2 cups micro greens (or pea shoots)

DRESSING

2 tablespoons minced fresh cilantro

2 tablespoons minced fresh basil

Zest of 1 lemon

3 tablespoons lemon juice

¼ cup extra virgin olive oil

1 tablespoon maple syrup

2 teaspoons prepared mustard of choice

Sea salt and freshly ground pepper

In large bowl, combine kohlrabi and beets. Cut scallions into pieces that match the length of the other julienned ingredients and julienne. Add to salad along with micro greens and toss to combine.

In separate bowl, whisk together cilantro, basil, lemon zest, lemon juice, olive oil, maple syrup and mustard. Season to taste with salt and pepper and pour over salad. Toss to evenly coat and serve.

SERVES 6

Note: Grow your own micro greens in ½-inch moist potting soil in a container with drainage (look for flats for growing seedlings at your local nursery). Sprinkle with seed mix of choice and top by sifting a thin layer of potting soil over the seeds. Place on a drip tray, water gently and place in full sun. Keep evenly moist and snip greens near base of stem when leaves unfold (2–3 weeks depending on seed variety and growing conditions).

Arugula and Mint Salad with Roasted Rhubarb and Lemon Maple Dressing

I CAN'T RESIST RHUBARB and always end up buying more than I need. My family expects me to use rhubarb in tarts and crisps, so when I first served it roasted they were skeptical. One bite and they were convinced. The combination of sweet, tart, bitter and sour in this recipe is unexpected and always a huge hit.

DRESSING

2   tablespoons lemon juice
1   tablespoon extra virgin olive oil
1   tablespoon maple syrup
Sea salt and freshly ground pepper

SALAD

2   cups cut-up rhubarb (½-inch pieces)
2   tablespoons maple syrup
⅛   teaspoon ground cardamom
6   cups arugula
1   cup mint leaves
¼   cup toasted pine nuts

Preheat oven to 350°F. Line baking sheet with parchment paper.

In small bowl, whisk together lemon juice, olive oil and maple syrup. Season to taste with salt and pepper and set dressing aside.

In separate bowl, combine rhubarb, maple syrup and cardamom. Stir to evenly coat and pour onto baking sheet. Roast 10 minutes or until rhubarb is just soft. Remove from oven and set aside to cool slightly.

In a large bowl, toss together arugula and mint leaves. Add dressing and toss to coat. Transfer to individual serving plates or one large platter, top with roasted rhubarb and toasted pine nuts and serve.

SERVES 4

Sugar Snap Peas with Orange Ginger Dressing

MY YOUNGER DAUGHTER THINKS OF SUGAR SNAP PEAS as candy from the farm. She eats them straight out of the bag, usually before we even get them home. Something this delicious requires no recipe at all, but just in case, here's a preparation as sweet and simple as sugar snap peas themselves.

---

4   cups sugar snap peas, strings removed

2   tablespoons extra virgin olive oil

1   teaspoon grated fresh ginger

3   tablespoons freshly squeezed orange juice

1   tablespoon maple syrup

1   tablespoon chopped fresh mint leaves

3   scallions, chopped

Pinch of coarse sea salt

Place sugar snap peas in bowl and bring kettle of water to boil. Pour boiling water over peas, soak 10 seconds or until peas are bright green, then drain into colander. Rinse under cold water, drain well and pat dry. Return to bowl and set aside.

In small pan over medium heat, sauté ginger in olive oil for 1 minute. Add orange juice and maple syrup and sauté 1 minute longer. Remove from heat and stir in mint and scallions.

Pour mixture over sugar snap peas and toss to combine. Sprinkle with coarse sea salt and serve.

SERVES 4

Kale Caesar Salad with Arame

WHEN MY RECIPE FOR RAW KALE CONFETTI SALAD came out in *Clean Start,* I demoed it at nearly every event for a year. I love raw kale, but even I was ready for a change. This Caesar twist features the super-nutrition of sea vegetables and is just the change I needed to keep me coming back for more raw kale salad.

CAESAR DRESSING

2	tablespoons extra virgin olive oil
2	tablespoons lemon juice
1	tablespoon tahini
1	large garlic clove, peeled
1	tablespoon capers
1	teaspoon whole-grain mustard
1	teaspoon chickpea miso

SALAD

¼	cup dried arame
1	large bunch kale (variety of choice)
⅛	teaspoon sea salt
¼	cup roasted sunflower seeds

In small bowl, whisk together olive oil, lemon juice and tahini. Use garlic press to crush garlic and add to dressing. Use garlic press again to crush capers and add to dressing. Add mustard and miso and whisk to combine all ingredients. Set dressing aside.

Place arame in bowl, cover with water and set aside to reconstitute.

Prepare kale by removing tough stems (not necessary for all varieties) and tearing into bite-size pieces. Place in large bowl and sprinkle with sea salt. Use hands to massage leaves until they break down and soften (kale will reduce significantly).

Pour dressing over kale and fold to coat all leaves. Drain soaking arame, press out excess water and add to kale. Fold to evenly incorporate into salad. Top with sunflower seeds and serve.

SERVES 4

SERVING SUGGESTIONS
Serve as is or dress salad with toppings such as sliced avocado, minced red onion, great northern beans, toasted pine nuts or grilled salmon.

Asparagus Salad with Meyer Lemon and Herbs

THERE ARE MANY COMBINATIONS OF BABY GREENS that set the stage perfectly for this salad. Some of my favorites include arugula, mustard greens, mizuna, watercress, kale, endive and mint. Experiment with your own favorites…and maybe discover some new ones.

1	bunch asparagus
2	cups boiling water
¼	cup thinly sliced red radishes
½	orange bell pepper, chopped
2	tablespoons minced red onion
1	tablespoon chopped fresh chives
2	cups baby greens of choice
1	avocado, pitted, peeled and chopped

Chive flowers as garnish

VINAIGRETTE

¼	cup extra virgin olive oil

Zest of 1 Meyer lemon

2	tablespoons Meyer lemon juice
1	tablespoon red wine vinegar
1	tablespoon chopped fresh dill
1	tablespoon chopped fresh mint
2	teaspoons maple syrup
1	tablespoon mustard seeds

Sea salt and freshly ground pepper

Bend asparagus near bottom of stalks to break off dried ends at natural breaking point. Discard ends and cut remaining stalks on an angle into 1-inch pieces. Place in bowl. Pour boiling water over asparagus, blanch 30 seconds or until bright green and drain.

Place blanched asparagus in bowl and add radishes, bell pepper, onion, chives and greens.

In small bowl, combine olive oil, lemon zest, lemon juice, vinegar, dill, mint and maple syrup. In small skillet over medium heat, toast mustard seeds until they start to pop. Remove from heat, transfer to mortar and use pestle to grind about half of seeds. Transfer to dressing and whisk together all ingredients. Season to taste with sea salt and pepper.

Pour dressing over salad and toss. Set aside to marinate 10 minutes. Toss before serving and garnish with avocado and chive flowers.

SERVES 6

Asparagus with Seared Shiitake Mushrooms and Ramps

MOTHER NATURE SCORED BIG POINTS WITH ME when she provided asparagus, shiitakes and ramps all in the same season. I often feel like I should highlight seasonal delicacies in their own dish, but who am I to mess with this trifecta of spring?

1	bunch asparagus (about 1 pound)
1	bunch ramps (about ¼ pound)
2	tablespoons extra virgin olive oil, plus more for drizzling
½	pound shiitake mushrooms, stemmed and thinly sliced
2	tablespoons tamari
Sea salt and freshly ground pepper	

Bend asparagus near bottom of stalks to break off dried ends at natural breaking point. Discard ends and cut remaining stalks on an angle into 2-inch pieces. Trim ramps and discard root ends. Separate greens from white bulbs, but keep greens whole and set aside. Halve bulbs lengthwise.

In large cast iron skillet over medium-high heat, sauté mushrooms in 2 tablespoons olive oil for 5 minutes, stirring only occasionally so mushrooms sear but don't burn. When mushrooms are browned, drizzle with tamari and sauté until mushroom are well seared (about 2 minutes longer). Transfer to bowl and set aside but keep skillet over heat.

Place sliced ramp bulbs in hot skillet and sear. If pan is dry, add 1 tablespoon water to deglaze pan and steam ramps. When soft, remove from heat and place in bowl with shiitakes.

Add asparagus to skillet and sear 1 minute. Add 1 tablespoon water and cook until asparagus is bright green and just tender (2–3 minutes). Fold in ramp greens and remove from heat. Transfer to serving dish, drizzle with olive oil and season to taste with salt and pepper. Top with mushrooms and seared ramps and serve.

SERVES 4

Roasted Carrot and Beet Salad with Baby Kale

THESE ARE NOT MY GRANDMOTHER'S cooked carrots! Together with beets, they satisfy the void left from winter's sweet roasted squashes and help me transition to spring's cleansing raw herbs and baby greens.

1½ teaspoons cumin seeds

1 pound carrots

4 small beets, peeled and cut into wedges

1 large orange, unpeeled, cut into 8 wedges

2 tablespoons extra virgin olive oil

1 tablespoon apple cider vinegar

¼ teaspoon sea salt

2 tablespoons fresh thyme leaves

4 cups baby kale

1 avocado, peeled, pitted and sliced

¼ cup chopped chives (with flowers if available)

¼ cup roasted sunflower seeds

DRESSING

3 tablespoons extra virgin olive oil

1 tablespoon lemon juice

1 tablespoon red wine vinegar

1 teaspoon maple syrup

⅛ teaspoon sea salt

Freshly ground pepper

Preheat oven to 400°F.

In small skillet over medium heat, dry-roast cumin seeds until fragrant (about 3 minutes). Remove from heat, transfer to mortar and grind with pestle. Set aside.

ROASTING VEGETABLES AND CITRUS

Halve carrots lengthwise (and quarter larger carrots). Place in baking dish and add beets, orange wedges, olive oil, cider vinegar, salt and thyme. Add 1 teaspoon cumin and toss until all ingredients are coated. Roast uncovered 45 minutes or until beets are tender throughout.

MAKING DRESSING

Pick orange wedges out of roasted vegetables, squeeze juice into separate bowl and discard oranges. Add any juices from baking dish and set vegetables aside. Add 3 tablespoons olive oil, lemon juice, red wine vinegar, maple syrup, sea salt and remaining cumin. Whisk to combine and season to taste with pepper.

FINISHING SALAD

In large bowl, combine baby kale, avocado and chives. Add dressing and toss to combine. Transfer roasted vegetables to serving dish and top with dressed greens. Sprinkle with sunflower seeds, dress with chive flowers and serve.

SERVES 4 as a main dish (8 as side salad)

VARIATION
Substitute pea shoots/tendrils for baby kale for a lighter finished dish.

Roasted Baby Artichokes with Tarragon Oil

BABY ARTICHOKES ARE SO MUCH EASIER TO PREPARE than their more mature relatives. With no choke to remove and no individual leaves to snip, you too will soon be bypassing the full-size artichokes.

¼ cup extra virgin olive oil

2 garlic cloves, sliced

1 tablespoon fresh tarragon leaves

Pinch of red pepper flakes

1 lemon, halved

6 cups water

16 baby artichokes

Coarse sea salt and freshly ground pepper

Preheat oven to 400°F.

Heat olive oil in small skillet over low heat. Add garlic and sauté until fragrant (about 2 minutes). Add tarragon and use a wooden spoon to press leaves into pan so they release their essence. Add pepper flakes, remove from heat and set aside.

Fill a bowl with cold water. Squeeze juice from one lemon half into water. Working one artichoke at a time, slice off and discard top one-third. Immediately rub cut edge with remaining lemon half. Pull off tough outer leaves until you reach tender light green leaves (it may feel like you're peeling more than necessary, but darker leaves will remain tough). Peel stem, trim and discard end of stem and halve artichoke lengthwise. Rub with lemon and place in lemon water. Repeat until all artichokes are prepared.

Drain lemon water and pat artichokes dry. Return artichokes to bowl. Strain olive oil through a fine-mesh strainer to remove solids and drizzle infused oil over artichokes. Season to taste with salt and pepper and toss to coat. Transfer to a baking sheet and roast 15 minutes on each side (30 minutes total) or until crispy on the outside and tender in the middle (roasting time will vary according to size of artichokes). Remove from oven and serve.

Note: Infused oil can be prepared ahead of time and store in an airtight container out of direct sunlight for up to 1 week.

SERVES 4

Sarah's Dandelion Thai Curry

MY OLDER DAUGHTER IS QUITE A COOK, insisting on making up her own recipes (just like her mom). As I was writing this book, Sarah mastered the fine art of curry. This is *her* recipe, but uses an ingredient that I requested—super-nutritional, liver-healing dandelion greens.

1   tablespoon virgin coconut oil

1   yellow onion, chopped

5   garlic cloves, minced

1   2-inch piece fresh ginger, peeled and julienned

1   2-inch piece fresh turmeric root, grated (or 2 teaspoons ground)

1   teaspoon five-spice powder

1   teaspoon ground cumin

¼   teaspoon cayenne

1   teaspoon sea salt

1   cup vegetable stock

1¼   cups whole coconut milk

2   tablespoons peanut butter

1   large sweet potato, peeled and cubed (¾-inch)

1   red bell pepper, stemmed and seeded

1½   cups chopped fresh pineapple

2   cups chopped dandelion leaves

¼   cup chopped fresh cilantro

Melt coconut oil in large Dutch oven over medium-low heat. Add onion and garlic and sauté 3 minutes. Stir in ginger, turmeric, five-spice powder, cumin, cayenne and sea salt and stir to combine. Add vegetable stock, coconut milk and peanut butter and whisk to dissolve peanut butter. Bring to simmer, fold in sweet potato, cover and cook until sweet potatoes are soft (about 10 minutes).

Remove lid from Dutch oven and mash one-quarter of the sweet potatoes to thicken sauce. Slice red pepper into long thin strips and then in half and fold into curry along with pineapple. Stir in dandelion leaves and remove curry from heat. Garnish with cilantro and serve.

SERVES 4

SERVING SUGGESTION
Serve over Steamed Purple Sticky Rice *(page 66)*.

Grilled Bok Choy with Spicy Apricot Sauce

AFTER A LONG, COLD WINTER, the mere suggestion of warmer weather makes me want to cook everything on the grill just outside the kitchen door. The cleanup is nothing, the smoky taste is amazing, and it takes practically no time. What could possibly be better?

1	tablespoon tamari
1	tablespoon lime juice
1	tablespoon apricot jam
½	teaspoon grated fresh ginger
⅛	teaspoon red pepper flakes
1½	pounds baby bok choy
1	tablespoon extra virgin olive oil
	Sea salt and freshly ground pepper
¼	cup chopped scallions or chives

Preheat grill to medium-high.

In small bowl, whisk together tamari, lime juice, apricot jam, ginger and pepper flakes and set aside.

Wash and dry bok choy and halve lengthwise, keeping root end connected. Place on platter, drizzle with olive oil and toss to coat evenly. Season with salt and pepper and lay individual pieces of bok choy on an angle on grill. Sear 2 minutes (or until you achieve nice grill lines), flip and grill 2 minutes longer or until bok choy stems are just soft with blackened grill lines.

Remove from heat and place bok choy in serving dish. Pour sauce evenly over bok choy, top with scallions and serve.

Note: I like to heat the front burner of my grill to medium-high and the far burner to low. Then I place the bok choy with their stem ends over the high-heat burner, and the leafy ends over the medium-low burner.

SERVES 4

Sautéed Fiddleheads

MY BROTHER KNEW THE DELIGHT OF FIDDLEHEADS long before I did. I tried and tried, but wasn't sold until I discovered the secret of presoaking. Not only does a cold bath wash away their bitter leaves, but it makes this foraged delicacy super-crispy, delicious and a must-have whenever they're available.

---

1 pound fiddleheads

1 tablespoon extra virgin olive oil

4 garlic cloves, minced

⅛ teaspoon red pepper flakes

Sea salt

Place fiddleheads in bowl, cover with cold water and swish with hands to remove brown leaves and miscellaneous pieces. Drain dirty water and repeat until water is clean. Fill bowl one final time, allow fiddleheads to soak 10 minutes and drain thoroughly. (Fiddleheads can soak for most of the day if that helps with timing your meal prep.)

Bring 1 inch of water to boil in medium pot with steamer rack. Steam fiddleheads for 3–4 minutes. Remove from steamer and set aside.

In large skillet over medium-low heat, sauté garlic in olive oil until soft (about 2 minutes). Add fiddleheads and sauté until just bright green (1–2 minutes). Be careful not to overcook or fiddleheads will turn brown. Remove from heat and toss with pepper flakes. Season to taste with sea salt and serve.

Note: For more al dente fiddleheads, sauté without steaming first.

SERVES 4

Rainbow Chard with Sweet Peas

DEEP GREEN LEAVES OR COLORFUL STEMS — it's hard to determine which make rainbow chard more special. If you're one who likes to cut off and discard the stems of dark leafy greens, rainbow chard's stems in orange, pink, yellow and red are guaranteed to change your mind.

2   cups sweet peas in the pod (to yield ½–¾ cup shelled)

3   cups boiling water

2   large bunches rainbow Swiss chard

1   tablespoon extra virgin olive oil

3   garlic cloves, thinly sliced

3   spring onions, sliced into thin rounds

Sea salt and freshly ground pepper

1   tablespoon chopped fresh dill (optional)

Shell peas and place in heatproof bowl. Pour boiling water over peas, blanch 10 seconds or until peas are just bright green. Drain, rinse with cold water and set aside.

Separate chard leaves and stems. Chop stems into equal-size pieces (about ¼ inch in width) and coarsely chop leaves.

In large cast iron skillet over medium heat, sauté garlic and onions in olive oil until soft (about 2 minutes). Add chard stems and sauté 1 minute longer. Fold in greens, continue sautéing and folding until just wilted. Remove from heat and add peas and dill (if using). Season with plenty of salt and pepper and serve warm.

Note: Enjoy this dish year-round by substituting frozen peas for fresh.

SERVES 4

Apricot Millet with Sage and Dill

DRIED APRICOTS ADD A TOUCH OF SWEETNESS to recipes (and are relatively low on the glycemic index). I keep them in the house for snacking, but adding them to whole grains can turn an otherwise plain dish into something special. Just a touch of fresh sage and this recipe tastes like it's straight from the garden.

---

10 unsulfured, unsweetened dried apricots

2¼ cups boiling water

1 cup millet

3 tablespoons extra virgin olive oil

6 shallots, chopped (about 1¼ cups)

1 tablespoon minced fresh sage

½ cup roasted sunflower seeds

Sea salt and freshly ground pepper

2 tablespoons chopped fresh dill

Chop apricots and place in heatproof medium bowl. Pour on boiling water and soak 30 minutes to soften fruit and infuse water. Use a slotted spoon to remove apricots. Reserve soaking liquid, chop apricots and set both aside.

Rinse millet, place in dry Dutch oven over medium heat and sauté lightly to toast (about 4 minutes). Add apricot-infused water and bring to boil. Reduce heat and simmer covered until all liquid is absorbed (about 25 minutes). Remove from heat and set aside to cool slightly before fluffing.

In skillet over medium-low heat, sauté shallots in 1 tablespoon olive oil until translucent (about 4 minutes). Add sage and apricots, sauté 1 minute longer to heat through and remove from heat.

Fluff millet and fold in shallot mixture. Add sunflower seeds, drizzle with remaining 2 tablespoons olive oil and fold to combine ingredients. Fold in fresh dill, season to taste with sea salt and pepper and serve.

SERVES 6

Grilled Ramps and Spring Vegetables over Lemon Parsley Quinoa

THE SEASON FOR RAMPS IS WAY TOO SHORT and you definitely don't want to miss out. I created this recipe specifically to highlight the ramps, but we enjoy this lemony quinoa long after ramp season is over.

1 cup quinoa

1½ cups water

1 orange bell pepper

12 ramps (or 2 leeks)

1 bunch asparagus

2 tablespoons extra virgin olive oil

Sea salt and freshly ground pepper

DRESSING

1 teaspoon mustard seeds

Zest of 1 lemon

2 tablespoons lemon juice

¼ cup extra virgin olive oil

¼ cup chopped fresh flat-leaf parsley

¼ teaspoon sea salt

Freshly ground pepper

Place quinoa in fine-mesh strainer and rinse well. Place in pot or rice cooker with water. Bring to boil and simmer covered until water is absorbed (about 15 minutes). Remove from heat and set aside to cool slightly before fluffing.

Preheat grill to high.

Cut bell pepper lengthwise into thick strips and place on tray ready for grilling. Peel and discard root ends from ramps and place on tray. (If using leeks, trim and discard root end and dark green tops and cut leek lengthwise into sections about the same width as asparagus.) Bend asparagus near bottom of stalks to break off dried ends at natural breaking point and place stalks on tray.

Drizzle 2 tablespoons olive oil over all vegetables. Sprinkle with sea salt and plenty of pepper and place on grill. Sear each side of each vegetable 2–3 minutes or until just soft with dark grill lines (time will vary according to size of vegetables). Remove from heat and set aside.

In small skillet over medium heat, dry-roast mustard seeds until lightly browned and fragrant. Remove from heat and gently grind using mortar and pestle. Transfer to small bowl and add lemon zest and juice, olive oil, parsley and sea salt. Whisk to combine and season to taste with pepper.

Fluff quinoa and drizzle dressing over top. Fold to incorporate and transfer to serving platter. Top with grilled vegetables and serve.

SERVES 4

Steamed Purple Sticky Rice

IT'S IMPOSSIBLE NOT LOVE A VARIETY OF RICE that is traditionally eaten as a dessert. Purple sticky rice is light, sweet, nutty and a beautiful deep purple. It's a hit all on its own. I don't do a thing to dress it up — just steam and serve, unless you're looking for a killer breakfast!

1½ cups purple sticky rice
Water

BREAKFAST OPTION

½ cup whole coconut milk
1 tablespoon maple syrup
¼ cup fruit (fresh, dried or frozen)
¼ cup toasted almonds
Pinch of sea salt

Rinse rice until water runs clear. Place in bowl and cover well with water. Soak overnight or as long as 24 hours.

Fit pot with steamer or wire-mesh basket that can hold grain above boiling water.

Fill pot with enough water to rise just below steamer or wire-mesh basket and bring to boil. Drain rice and place in basket (if steamer rack openings are too large to hold rice, place rice in cheesecloth, pull up sides and twist top loosely, leaving room in pouch for rice to expand). Cover and steam 30 minutes (check occasionally to make sure pot does not run out of water). Remove cover, fold rice (or flip cheesecloth pouch) and steam covered 20 more minutes or until rice is soft. Remove from heat and serve.

BREAKFAST OPTION

Transfer steamed rice to serving or individual bowls. Heat coconut milk in small pan over medium heat. Stir in maple syrup and remove from heat. Pour over rice, top with fruit, almonds and sea salt, and serve.

SERVES 4

Warm Fava Beans and Rice with Lemon and Herbs

FAVA BEANS ARE THE PERFECT REASON to enlist help in the kitchen. My girls are much more likely to try something if they helped make it, and this dish goes super-fast with more than two hands for peeling beans. More importantly, everyone appreciates even more the love that goes into a meal when they know firsthand what went into the prep.

---

1 cup brown basmati rice

2 cups water

Pinch of sea salt

2 pounds fava beans in pods (to yield 2 cups shelled)

3 tablespoons extra virgin olive oil

⅓ cup finely chopped red onion

2 garlic cloves, minced

¼ cup minced fresh dill

¼ cup minced fresh mint

2 tablespoons lemon juice

Sea salt and freshly ground pepper

Place rice in pot or rice cooker with water and sea salt. Bring to boil, reduce heat and simmer covered until liquid is absorbed (about 25 minutes). Remove from heat and set aside.

Remove favas from pods (discard pods). Bring 2 inches water to boil in medium pot with steamer rack. Steam favas 1 minute. Remove from heat, rinse under cold water and set aside for 5 minutes or until skins start to shrivel. Pinch open skin at end and peel beans. Discard inedible peels and set favas aside.

In small skillet over medium heat, sauté onion and garlic in olive oil until just soft (about 2 minutes). Add dill and mint and sauté 1 minute longer. Stir in lemon juice. Remove from heat and fold in favas.

Fluff rice and fold in onion-fava mixture. Season with plenty of sea salt and ground pepper and fold one more time to combine all ingredients. Serve warm.

SERVES 4

Tempeh Reuben Casserole

IF YOU'VE EVER EATEN THE TEMPEH REUBEN at River Valley Market in Northampton, Massachusetts, you know exactly why I went home and immediately created this recipe.

DRESSING

¼   cup grapeseed oil mayonnaise

3   tablespoons ketchup, store-bought or home-made (*page 227*)

3   tablespoons sweet pickle relish

Hot sauce of choice

FILLING

1½   cups quartered fingerling or baby potatoes

4   tablespoons extra virgin olive oil

½   Vidalia onion, thinly sliced

12   ounces tempeh, cut into ½-inch strips

1½   cups sauerkraut, store-bought or homemade (*page 165*)

4   ounces shredded or sliced vegan Swiss-style cheese (optional)

TOPPING

¼   cup gluten-free breadcrumbs

½   teaspoon caraway seeds

1   teaspoon extra virgin olive oil

Pinch of sea salt

In small bowl, whisk together mayonnaise, ketchup and relish. Season to taste with hot sauce and set dressing aside.

Steam potatoes until soft and place in bottom of 8 x 8-inch baking dish. In cast iron skillet over medium heat, sauté onion in 1 tablespoon olive oil until soft and lightly browned (about 5 minutes). Remove from heat and spread onions over potatoes in casserole.

Add 2 tablespoons more olive oil to pan and increase heat to high. Add tempeh and sear until evenly browned and crisp (2–3 minutes per side). Remove from heat and arrange tempeh over potatoes and onions.

Preheat broiler to medium high.

Evenly spread dressing over tempeh. Top with sauerkraut, then cheese if desired and set aside.

In small skillet over low heat, dry-roast caraway seeds until fragrant (2–3 minutes). Transfer to mortar and use pestle to partially grind seeds. Transfer to small bowl and add breadcrumbs, olive oil and sea salt. Mix until crumbs are consistently moist and sprinkle over casserole.

Place casserole in oven and broil until cheese melts and breadcrumbs lightly brown. Remove from oven and serve.

SERVES 6

Roasted Asparagus and Fennel with Fava Beans

I LOVE THE CONTRAST of fresh steamed fava beans with savory roasted vegetables, all brought together with a hint of mint. I often serve this over polenta, pasta or a bed of arugula. When fresh fava beans aren't available, I toss in wedges of blood oranges instead. You just can't lose when you combine roasted asparagus and fennel.

2	pounds fava beans in pods (to yield 2 cups shelled)
2	bunches asparagus
1	fennel bulb, halved and cored
6	garlic cloves, peeled
2	tablespoons extra virgin olive oil
½	teaspoon coarse sea salt
1	teaspoon minced fresh mint
Freshly ground pepper	

Remove favas from pods and discard pods. Bring 2 inches water to boil in medium pot steamer rack. Steam favas 1 minute. Remove from heat, rinse under cold water and set aside for 5 minutes or until skins start to shrivel. Pinch open skin at end and peel beans. Discard inedible peels and set favas aside.

Preheat oven to 400°F.

Bend asparagus near bottom of stalks to break off dried ends at natural breaking point. Discard ends, cut remaining stalks on an angle into 2-inch pieces and place in large bowl. Slice fennel into thin wedges and add to bowl with asparagus. Add garlic cloves and drizzle with olive oil. Sprinkle with sea salt, toss to coat and spread on baking sheet.

Roast 20 minutes or until vegetables are tender and lightly browned. Remove from oven, lightly mash garlic and add prepared fava beans and mint. Toss to combine, season to taste with pepper and serve.

SERVES 4

Sprouted Lentil Salad with Dried Plums and Toasted Walnuts

THIS SALAD REQUIRES ADVANCE PLANNING to sprout the lentils, but minimum effort otherwise. Not only is it delicious, but it tastes much more like a splurge than a spring cleanse.

¼   cup black lentils

¼   cup French lentils

4   tablespoons extra virgin olive oil

2   tablespoons cold-pressed roasted pistachio oil

2   tablespoons apple cider vinegar

2   small shallots, minced

2   teaspoons maple syrup

Sea salt and freshly ground pepper

1   cup finely chopped pitted dried plums

1   cup toasted chopped walnuts

¼   cup plus 2 tablespoons chopped fresh cilantro

Combine lentils in bowl, cover well with water and soak 12 hours. Drain through wire-mesh sieve and rinse well. Rest sieve with lentils over bowl, cover with cheesecloth and set aside on counter to sprout. Total sprouting time is 3–5 days. During that time, rinse sprouts thoroughly and drain 2–3 times a day. When sprouted and ready to use, you should have 2 cups lentil sprouts with ¼- to ½-inch tails.

In small bowl, whisk together olive oil, pistachio oil, apple cider vinegar, shallots, maple syrup, and sea salt and pepper to taste. Set aside to allow flavors to develop and blend.

Transfer sprouts to bowl and add plums, walnuts and cilantro. Drizzle with dressing, toss to combine and serve.

SERVE 6

Great Northern Beans with Broccoli, Peas and Pistachio Pesto

RICH, CREAMY, TART AND DELICIOUS — what is there not to love about pesto? I know my family really loves this dish because they willingly give up enough pistachios to make the pesto.

PESTO

1   garlic clove, peeled

½   cup pistachios, toasted

1   cup firmly packed fresh flat-leaf parsley

1   cup firmly packed fresh basil or cilantro

Zest of 1 lemon

1   tablespoon lemon juice

¼   cup extra virgin olive oil

Sea salt

BEANS

1   tablespoon extra virgin olive oil

2–3 heads broccoli, cut into bite-size pieces (about 4 cups)

¼   cup warm water

1½ cups cooked great northern beans

½   cup shelled green peas

Sea salt and freshly ground pepper

To prepare pesto, drop garlic into running food processor to mince. Turn processor off, add pistachios and process nuts into meal. Add parsley, basil, lemon zest and lemon juice and process to combine. With processor running, pour in olive oil and continue processing until pesto is smooth. Season to taste with salt and set aside.

Heat olive oil in large cast iron skillet over medium-high heat. Add broccoli to skillet and sauté until bright green. With pan very hot, pour in ¼ cup water and steam broccoli the rest of the way until just tender. Fold in beans and two-thirds of pesto and continue sautéing 1–2 minutes to heat through. Add more pesto as desired (I use about three-quarters and my children use it all). Fold in peas and sauté until just bright green. Remove from heat, season to taste with salt and pepper and serve.

SERVES 4

VARIATION

To toss this dish with pasta, cook 8 ounces of gluten-free pasta of choice according to directions on package. Drain pasta, reserving ¼ cup cooking water. Add all of the pesto and the extra ¼ cup water to broccoli sauté. Fold to combine all ingredients and serve.

Red Lentil Patties with Garlic and Fresh Herbs

RED LENTILS RANK HIGH IN MY KITCHEN because they cook up in less than 15 minutes. These patties are a mother's dream—easy to make, beautiful to serve and perfect for leftovers.

1	cup red lentils
2½	cups vegetable stock or water
2	tablespoons extra virgin olive oil, plus more as needed
4	garlic cloves, peeled
1	cup chopped red onion
¼	cup chopped roasted red pepper
¼	cup chopped fresh herbs (parsley, basil, cilantro or any combination)
¼	teaspoon sea salt
	Freshly ground pepper
½	cup gluten-free bread or rice crumbs

Rinse and drain lentils and place in pot with vegetable stock or water. Bring to boil, reduce heat and simmer covered 15 minutes until lentils are mushy and all liquid is absorbed (you may want to leave lid cracked open slightly to prevent pot from boiling over). Remove from heat and set aside.

In large cast iron skillet, sauté garlic and onion in 1 tablespoon olive oil until soft (about 3 minutes). Add roasted red pepper and sauté 1 minute longer. Remove from heat and transfer mixture to a bowl. Add lentils, fold in herbs and sea salt, and season to taste with pepper. Gradually fold in breadcrumbs until batter is thick (you may not need all depending on how dry your lentils are) and set aside for 2–3 minutes to allow batter to thicken.

Drizzle cast iron skillet with 1 tablespoon olive oil. Scoop batter and roll into 1½-inch balls. Place in skillet and flatten into patties ½- to ¾-inch thick. Cook until crispy (4–5 minutes per side), transfer to baking sheet and cover to keep warm. Repeat with remaining batter until ingredients are used up and serve.

SERVES 6 (makes twelve 2½-inch patties)

Chocolate Chunk
Banana Loaves

EVERYONE SHOULD HAVE A BANANA BREAD RECIPE they love, and this recipe is it. High-protein, high-fiber and low-carb coconut flour makes this a decadent bread that's guilt-free and simply delicious

DRY INGREDIENTS

- ⅓ cup coconut flour
- ⅓ cup brown teff flour
- 2 teaspoons baking powder
- ½ teaspoon baking soda
- ¼ teaspoon sea salt
- ½ cup gluten-free dark chocolate chunks

WET INGREDIENTS

- 2 mashed ripe bananas (about a heaping ½ cup)
- ½ cup applesauce
- ½ cup maple syrup
- ¼ cup coconut oil, melted, plus more for greasing pans
- 1 teaspoon vanilla extract

Preheat oven to 350°F. Lightly grease two 5½ x 3½-inch loaf pans with coconut oil.

In large bowl, whisk together coconut flour, teff flour, baking powder, baking soda and sea salt. In separate bowl, whisk together all wet ingredients. Pour wet ingredients into dry and fold until just combined. Fold in chocolate chunks and divide evenly between loaf pans. Smooth tops with spatula and place in oven. Bake 45 minutes or until tops are browned.

Remove from oven and cool in pans on wire rack. Remove from pans and serve.

MAKES 2 mini loaves

Rhubarb Tart

IF YOU THINK RHUBARB SCREAMS FOR STRAWBERRIES, this tart will change your mind. Not that strawberries and rhubarb aren't a match made in heaven, but sometimes a girl buys rhubarb at the farm and forgets the strawberries. After this tart, I started "forgetting" the strawberries on purpose.

CRUST

2 cups almond flour/meal

Pinch of sea salt

2 tablespoons maple syrup

1 tablespoon virgin coconut oil, melted plus extra to grease pan

1 teaspoon almond extract

1 teaspoon lemon zest

FILLING

6 cups chopped rhubarb (½-inch pieces)

3 tablespoons maple syrup

⅛ teaspoon ground cinnamon

3 dashes of ground ginger

GLAZE

3 tablespoons seedless raspberry all-fruit jam

Zest of 1 lemon

1 tablespoon lemon juice

Preheat oven to 350°F. Grease a 9-inch tart pan with coconut oil.

PREPARING CRUST

In large bowl, combine almond flour and sea salt. In separate bowl, whisk together maple syrup, melted coconut oil, almond extract and lemon zest. Pour wet ingredients into dry and fold to combine. Transfer dough to tart pan and press to form crust. Bake 15 minutes or until golden brown. Remove from oven and, using the back of a wooden spoon, gently press down any puffed areas of crust. Set crust on wire rack to cool. Leave oven on for rhubarb.

PREPARING FILLING

Line rimmed baking sheet with parchment paper. In large bowl, toss rhubarb with maple syrup, cinnamon and ginger. Spread evenly on baking sheet and roast 15 minutes or until soft but not mushy. Remove from oven and set aside.

FINISHING TART

Use a slotted spatula to transfer roasted rhubarb to tart shell. Pour any remaining rhubarb-roasting juices into a small skillet. Add jam, lemon zest and lemon juice to skillet and whisk over medium-low heat until liquid. Spoon glaze evenly over rhubarb and allow to set until ready to serve.

MAKES one 9-inch tart

Dark Chocolate and Blood Orange Truffles

SOMETIMES IT FEELS LIKE THERE'S A CELEBRATION every week of spring—Easter, Passover, Mother's Day and countless birthdays. I save this recipe for when I want something extra special. You know, like every weekend.

¼ cup cashew butter

2 tablespoons raw cacao powder

1 tablespoon virgin coconut oil, melted

3 tablespoons maple syrup

3 tablespoons freshly squeezed blood orange juice

½ teaspoon orange extract

¼ teaspoon vanilla extract

2 tablespoons coconut flour

¾ cup gluten-free dark chocolate

¼ teaspoon coarse sea salt or 1 tablespoon unsweetened dried shredded coconut

In small bowl, combine cashew butter, cacao powder, coconut oil, maple syrup, blood orange juice, orange extract and vanilla extract. Use spatula to blend, pressing firmly into mixture to break up clumps and yield smooth batter. Fold in coconut flour and blend until smooth. Cover bowl and refrigerate 1 hour.

Line baking sheet with parchment paper. Remove mixture from refrigerator, scoop by the teaspoon and press together to form balls. Place chocolate in small skillet or double boiler over low heat and stir until melted and smooth. Drop one ball at a time into chocolate, spoon chocolate over the top to coat and carefully lift ball from the bottom using a fork and place on parchment-lined baking sheet. When chocolate is almost firm but still slightly shiny, sprinkle top with a few grains of coarse sea salt or shredded coconut. Set aside or refrigerate until firm before serving.

Note: Top with pink sea salt for an extra special finish. If blood oranges are unavailable, substitute 3 tablespoons pomegranate juice.

MAKES about 20 truffles

Mixed Berry and Toasted Almond Crumble

THIS IS MY GO-TO RECIPE after a successful berry-picking excursion My family likes this crumble for dessert, but I prefer it as leftovers the next morning for breakfast, heated slightly and served with a little almond or coconut milk poured over the top.

6   cups berries
(my favorite combo is
blueberries, raspberries
and blackberries)

2   tablespoons maple syrup

Zest of 1 lemon

1   cup gluten-free rolled oats

½   cup teff flour
(ivory preferred)

½   cup sliced almonds, toasted

¼   cup coconut palm sugar

⅛w   teaspoon sea salt

¼   cup virgin coconut oil,
melted, plus extra
to grease baking dish

¼   cup maple syrup

1   teaspoon vanilla extract

Preheat oven to 350°F. Lightly grease an 8 x 8-inch baking dish with coconut oil.

In large bowl, fold together berries, maple syrup and lemon zest, and pour into prepared dish.

In same bowl, combine oats, teff flour, almonds, coconut palm sugar and sea salt. In separate bowl, combine coconut oil, maple syrup and vanilla. Drizzle over oat mixture and fold to combine. Spoon half of oat mixture over berries and use a spatula to lift berries slightly to partially incorporate crumble mixture. Sprinkle remaining topping over berries and bake 30 minutes or until berries start to burst and topping is crisp.

Remove from heat and set aside to cool slightly before serving.

SERVES 8

SERVING SUGGESTIONS
Delicious topped with vanilla, almond or coffee coconut milk ice cream and a sprig of fresh mint.

Dark Chocolate Cookies with Coarse Sea Salt and Cacao Nibs

I AM DEFINITELY A GIRL WHO FAVORS SALT over sweet. Add the bitterness of cacao and I am over the moon. Here, I use olive oil to bring out the richness of the cacao even more, and the result is a sweet, rich and decadent cookie with a hint of salt. Now *that* is my kind of cookie.

DRY INGREDIENTS

1   cup brown teff flour
1   cup almond flour/meal
½   cup raw cacao powder
¼   cup coconut palm sugar
1   teaspoon baking soda
¼   teaspoon sea salt

WET INGREDIENTS

½   cup applesauce
½   cup plus 2 tablespoons maple syrup
¼   cup almond butter
2   tablespoons extra virgin olive oil
2   teaspoons vanilla extract

TOPPING

Coarse sea salt
Cacao nibs

Preheat oven to 350°F. Line baking sheet with parchment paper.

In medium bowl, whisk together all dry ingredients (cacao powder can be stubborn, so make sure all chunks are broken so you don't have to overmix the batter later). In separate small bowl, whisk together all wet ingredients. Add wet ingredients to dry and fold with spatula to evenly combine and work into batter.

Scoop by heaping tablespoon and place evenly spaced on prepared baking sheet. Top each cookie with a pinch of sea salt and cacao nibs and gently press into batter. Bake 12 minutes. Remove from heat and set aside to cool…or devour immediately from the oven like we do!

MAKES 2 dozen cookies

Carrot Cake

CATHERINE HAD BEEN USING MY COOKBOOKS for years before she emailed me requesting a carrot cake recipe. Her email was just the nudge I needed to create this recipe, so we all have Catherine to thank!

4   Medjool dates, pitted

2   cups shredded carrots

1   cup minced fresh pineapple

1   cup chopped toasted walnuts

1   cup raisins

DRY INGREDIENTS

¾   cup ivory or brown teff flour

¾   cup coconut flour

1   tablespoon ground cinnamon

2   teaspoons baking powder

1½   teaspoons baking soda

½   teaspoon sea salt

WET INGREDIENTS

1   cup virgin coconut oil, melted, plus more for greasing pan

1   cup maple syrup

½   cup applesauce

2   teaspoons vanilla extract

FROSTING

1½   cups coconut butter

¾   cup whole coconut milk

¾   cup maple syrup

1   cup chopped toasted walnuts

BAKING CAKE

Preheat oven to 350°F. Grease two 9-inch round springform pans with coconut oil and line the bottom of each pan with a round of parchment paper.

Place dates in small heatproof bowl and cover with boiling water. Soak 5 minutes, drain and squeeze to remove excess liquid. Place dates in large bowl with carrots, pineapple, walnuts and raisins. Use hands to mix and massage mashed date into other ingredients. Set aside.

In a separate bowl, whisk together all dry ingredients. And in a third bowl combine all wet ingredients. Add wet ingredients to dry and fold to combine. Pour this mixture into bowl with carrots and fold to evenly distribute all ingredients.

Divide batter evenly between 2 prepared pans, smooth tops and bake 40 minutes or until a toothpick inserted in center comes out clean. Remove from oven, place on wire rack and cool completely.

FINISHING CAKE

In food processor, whip together coconut butter, coconut milk and maple syrup until smooth. Carefully remove one cake from pan and place on cake plate. Spread half the frosting over the first layer. Remove second layer from pan and place on top of first. Spread top with remaining frosting, top with walnuts and serve.

MAKES one 9-inch double layer cake

SUMMER

RADIATING ENERGY FROM THE SUN

I feel its warmth on my back as I work in the garden, see its rays breaking through the forest as I hike, fight against its intensity as I run and bike, and enjoy its penetrating heat even just driving in my car or sitting on my front porch. With the sun's energy, everything flourishes in my garden and in my life. My spirit is lifted, my mood lightened and my good health supported. Like the plants around me, I stand tall to soak it all in. There is a fullness and spontaneity to summer that makes everything possible. A long bike ride, a full day of work, a visit to the farm and dinner with family and friends. Six months from now I'll be wondering how I fit it all in. And yet in summer, it flows easily. Impromptu activities and unexpected adventures make life rich and nourishing, and I haven't even gotten to the food! My visits to the farm connect me with my farmer and the community that the farm brings together. I revel over freshly-picked berries that stain my hands and teeth, juicy peaches I have to slurp as much as bite, and sweet tomatoes in every size and color, begging to be eaten with just a shaker of salt. I taste as I shop, thinking that the farm should weigh me when I arrive and then again when I leave, and charge me accordingly. It is summer after all. Who could possibly resist?

CONTENTS

Vitamin D and the Sun

I feel like the solar panels that stand in the field, tracking the movement of the sun, providing valuable energy to use and to store. The body's transformation of sunlight to usable vitamin D is critical to our health and well-being. Deficiency of vitamin D is linked to insufficient absorption of calcium and minerals and a number of health concerns ranging from osteoporosis and autoimmune diseases to diabetes, elevated blood pressure and a number of cancers.

Food is almost always the best source of vitamins and minerals. Vitamin D, however, is already naturally produced by the body but requires sunlight to convert it into a form that our bodies can use. Unfortunately, the ultraviolet rays of the sun that are essential to activate vitamin D conversion are the same harmful rays that cause us to slather on sunscreen day in and day out. As a result, a growing percentage of people are vitamin D deficient. While I've yet to find a clear solution to this dilemma, there are strategies that can help us walk the fine line between essential sun exposure and overexposure.

NATURAL SUN PROTECTION

The surest way to protect yourself from the sun's damaging rays is to avoid unprotected exposure to the sun from 10 am to 2 pm, when the sun is its strongest. This is not a bad time to get your vitamin D fix, as long as you are careful to limit your exposure (staying out only until skin is just barely pink). The time you'll need in the sun will vary depending on the time of day, the weather, the season, the color of your skin and how much tan you already have. Start with ten minutes of sun a day. Once your skin becomes light pink, longer exposure only puts you at greater risk for damage. If exposure is longer, wear a natural and safe sunscreen.

Here are some other strategies for safely enjoying time in the sun:

Fill your plate with foods that boost your body's natural defense against the sun. Look for foods rich in lycopene (tomatoes and watermelon), carotene (carrots and sweet potatoes), vitamin C (strawberries and bell peppers), flavonoids (dark chocolate and citrus), omega-3s (wild-caught salmon, walnuts and flaxseeds) and antioxidant-rich green tea, garlic, and dark leafy herbs and greens.

Avoid foods that create inflammation and weaken the immune system (particularly processed foods, sugar and artificial sweeteners, dairy, wheat and alcohol).

Wear protective clothing and a brimmed hat when in the direct sun.

For minimal sun protection, use organic virgin coconut oil directly on the skin for moisturizing with the added benefit of natural SPF4 protection.

Even if they claim to be "natural" and "organic", many sunscreens may still contain petrochemicals and synthetic ingredients linked to a host of health concerns. Check brands on Environmental Working Group's website (EWG.org) to ensure they don't contain harmful, endocrine-disrupting ingredients.

Keeping Cool

This is about turning on your body's built-in air-conditioning system with the foods that you eat. By focusing on the fruits and vegetables that grow seasonally and locally, we will naturally be more in balance with our environment—in summer and every season. Mother Nature gives us the plant medicine we need for health and balance. The challenge is to listen and follow her lead.

Equally important for keeping cool are the cooking techniques we employ. Intrinsically, we crave cooling and refreshing juicy raw fruits and vegetables in summer and slow-cooked soups and sauces in winter, and for good reason. The longer our food is cooked, the more warming effect it has on the body. Conversely, the less cooked, the more cooling and cleansing.

COOLING FOOD PREPARATION

Summer meals inevitably start with a basket full of produce, whether from my garden, the farm or the farmers market. I love picking each bean, selecting curly scapes of garlic and transporting delicate tomatoes to create recipes that nourish and satisfy. In summer, more than any other season, I want minimal preparation. If I wrote down recipes each time I made a meal, many would read simply...*Pick and eat.* More often than not, this is what my body likes best, too.

RAW

We're all familiar with raw fruits and vegetables, but also in the raw category are homemade juices, smoothies, sprouts and dehydrated foods. These super-cleansing foods are the most cooling, and don't require fancy and expensive equipment.

A basic blender will make a variety of fruit and vegetable juices and smoothies. Just blend your ingredients on high until they are as broken down as possible, then use cheesecloth to strain juice into a separate container. Drink as is or return to blender and combine with ice, liquid (almond milk, coconut water…) and as much remaining plant fiber as desired. Now you've turned your juice into a satisfying and cooling smoothie.

High-powered blenders that pulverize fruits and vegetables make smoothies much easier and serve a number of other uses. I love my Vitamix, and have heard only good things about Blendtec blenders as well. Less expensive options (like the NutriBullet and Magic Bullet) are becoming more and more available.

A dehydrator is another great appliance that allows us to make a variety of living raw foods, and is also a powerful and healthful tool for preserving the harvest. I use a dehydrator (or an oven set as low as 110°–125°) in the Fall section to make Kale Chips *(page 168)* and fruit leather *(page 208)*, but my dehydrator comes out in summer as well to dehydrate a variety of summer produce (especially herbs and tomatoes).

SPROUTED

Sprouting makes nutrients easier to absorb and digest and increases their nutritional value. Whether sprouting grains, legumes, nuts or seeds, soak them in water first to unlock their nutritional value. Then drain and bring to germination. When sprouts become visible, no further cooking is necessary. Just add them to your recipe and enjoy. Once at their peak, sprouts can either be refrigerated to slow the process or dehydrated to hold for later use. Soaking grains before cooking achieves some of this same benefit. While a short soak of an hour is not enough to sprout the grain, it is enough to eliminate water-soluble phytic acid and make grains easier to assimilate and digest (with the added benefit of requiring less water and time to cook).

LACTO-FERMENTED

Lacto-fermented foods are an incredible source of bioavailable probiotics and B vitamins. The beneficial bacteria they provide support everything from a healthy gut and digestion to overall immune strength and general health. (See Fall for more information on lacto-fermented foods.)

GRILLED

Cooking over high heat for a short time is a great way to bring out a food's taste and achieve a slightly cooked texture without overcooking and significantly reducing nutrients.

PAN SEARED

Similar to grilling, pan searing is cooking at high temperature for a short period of time. Searing gives foods a just-tender texture on the inside and a crisp and slightly browned finish on the outside.

BROILED

Another cooking method using high heat and a short cooking time. Broiling is particularly good for bringing out the natural juices of tomatoes and caramelizing a variety of fruits and vegetables.

Sharing Meals

Perhaps what I appreciate the most about summer, more than sunshine and fresh produce, is the sense of community that results from people living outside, coming together at farmers markets and enjoying the season. Meals are quick, easy and always improved by being shared. Not only does extra time with family and friends bring more laughter, joy and connection, but it makes mealtime an even greater adventure as we share recipes, family traditions and new ways to prepare a variety of seasonal favorites.

TAKING IT OUTDOORS

I favor both ends of the day in summer, rising early to exercise outdoors before the heat soars, and coming back together late in the day over a meal. Eating outdoors is one of my favorite mindfulness practices. Somehow the simple act of moving food outside changes a meal dramatically. Whether I set a beautiful table or just bring my plate out and sit on a blanket, I am much more likely to eat slowly, savor each bite, linger over my meal and feed all of my senses. The result? I chew more, connect more and am nourished more by my meal and shared mealtime.

As the season draws to an end and the nights get colder and darker, an outdoor fire extends the season and provides a whole new way of cooking and connecting. These meals provide us with the opportunity slow down, let down, and create traditions, rituals and memories. When we remember the colorful Swiss chard, the tangy tomatillos and the sweet beets that we enjoyed all summer long, our memories will be framed by these moments created around the food, and we will undoubtedly be healthier.

ON THE GO

Our summer diets present two challenges: fueling increased activity, and packing meals to eat away from home. Never more than in summer am I tempted by quick and easy packaged energy bars and snacks for extended exercise and road trips. Keeping a well-stocked pantry makes preparing for spontaneous outings much easier.

Make your own energy bars. Stock your pantry with a selection of nuts, seeds and superfoods to make no-bake bars a quick and easy option. Follow my NoNo Bar recipe *(page 272)* once, then use the same proportions but substitute your own favorite ingredients the next time. Wrap bars individually in parchment paper so you can grab and go.

Wrap up your meals. Tortillas, summer roll wrappers and nori are all great ways to turn last night's leftovers into a portable lunch on the go.

Be smoothie-ready. Super-refreshing, filling and nutritious smoothies come together quickly as long as you keep a selection of frozen fruit and berries on hand. Add nut or seed butter for extra protein, an avocado for healthy fats and some raw kale, spinach or cucumber to get your veggies in.

Dump and stir. Chop up vegetables, toss with cooked grains or beans (or both) and dress with your favorite vinaigrette. This advice was given to me to help me eat clean before I knew how to cook. It's gotten me this far, so it seems to work!

Dip in. Freshly cut vegetables are much more appealing when you have your own bean dip, aioli or freshly made pesto for dipping. Dips and spreads can turn an otherwise plain salad into a killer wrap!

Pack clean. Don't undo your efforts by packing your healthy meals in plastic. Opt for parchment paper, reusable pouches or heavy-gauge glass containers, especially when there's acidic lemon or lime involved.

Locally Grown

There are many local farmstands, pick-your-own farms and events that connect us with our local food system and support our local economy, but perhaps my favorite excursion is to the farmers market. There is nothing else quite like this homegrown showcase of the bounty of farmers, artisans and locally grown produce unique to a region. I never know what I'm going to discover, but I enjoy taking in the energy of the market as if it were a midday meal, and each week becoming more immersed and nourished by the sense of community that grows there.

It's also never too late to plant produce. Some produce, like lettuce and arugula, do well in spring and fall, while others flourish in summer's heat. Check your plant hardiness zone to learn what grows best during each part of the season, then go for it. I rotate crops all season long, some started as seeds indoors, others planted directly as seedlings. Toward the end of the season I broadcast leftover seeds (manually sprinkling them over my garden) as cover crop to nourish and protect my soil throughout winter.

If you don't have a yard, a deck, or a rooftop to grow your own food, community gardens offer another option with a number of benefits. Not only are they often fenced in and have access to water, but you're likely to discover a whole new community of gardeners and friends from whom to learn and share. Schools are also a great place to find gardens and usually need caretakers over the summer while their students and faculty are on vacation.

Locally grown produce is much more likely to be available at your local grocery store during the growing season. And of course, if it's not, ask. The more you know about the source of your food, no matter where you purchase it, the more empowered you will be to make healthy choices.

Ultimately, the more we eat the foods that grow around us in season, the more we will be in balance with our environment. Locally grown food is a powerful way to take advantage of the health-giving power of produce to maintain good health and well-being for our communities, our economy, our environment and ourselves.

HOLDING ON TO SUMMER

Summer offers a sensory experience like no other season.
The beauty of the land, the chirping of crickets, the buzzing of bees, the twinkling of stars,
the smell of fresh air and sweet flowers, the soft leaves of mint and the prickly branches of berries…
all providing as much nourishment as the bounty of fresh and delicious produce. The season is short,
but I live it with gusto, taking in as much as possible, breathing it into my soul
and hoping that it will hold me until the season comes around again.

Juices and Smoothies

JUICES AND SMOOTHIES ARE A CLEANSING and refreshing way to get your vitamins and minerals, and you don't need to have an expensive machine to enjoy both. A basic blender will break down most vegetables to make a smoothie, and you can strain out the fiber for a simpler juice.

KALE CELERY PEACH

- 1 cup firmly packed chopped kale (stemmed)
- ½ lime (skin and all)
- 1 celery stalk, chopped
- 1 banana, peeled
- ¾ cup frozen sliced peaches
- 2 tablespoons maple syrup
- 1 cup ice cubes
- ½ cup rice milk, water or coconut water

HONEYDEW GINGER BASIL

- 4 cups honeydew cubes
- ⅓ cup packed fresh basil
- ½ lime (skin and all)
- 1 heaping teaspoon grated fresh ginger
- 1 cup ice cubes

CARROT GINGER BEET

- 1 carrot, chopped
- 1 golden beet, peeled and chopped
- 1 orange, peeled
- 2 teaspoons grated fresh ginger

Juice of ½ lemon

- 1 cup ice cubes
- ¾ cup water or iced hibiscus tea

Place solid ingredients in high-powered blender and process until smooth. Use tamper to push ingredients down to blade to be blended. Add liquid ingredients accordingly and process on high until consistent and smooth. Pour into 2 glasses and serve.

To enjoy as a juice, drape cheesecloth over a bowl and pour in smoothie. Pull up sides of cloth, twist ends and squeeze juice into bowl. Pour into glasses and serve.

VARIATIONS

To give your smoothie extra nutritional punch, add any number of super-nutritionals including presoaked flax or chia seeds, Basic Chia Pudding *(page 18)* protein powder, spirulina powder, chlorella powder or maca powder.

Multicolored Tomato Salsa

THIS FRESH SALSA MIRRORS the bins of multicolored heirloom tomatoes at the farmers market that I love so much. I use tomatoes in all shapes, sizes, colors and texture to create this salsa, which is as pleasing to the eye as it is to eat.

1½ cups diced tomatoes (mixed varieties and colors)

2 tomatillos, husked and diced

¼ cup finely chopped red onion

1 jalapeño, seeded and minced

2 garlic cloves, minced

2 tablespoons chopped fresh cilantro

1 tablespoon lime juice

1 tablespoon extra virgin olive oil

Pinch of sea salt

Freshly ground pepper

In bowl, combine tomatoes, tomatillos, onion, jalapeños, garlic and cilantro and fold to evenly distribute ingredients. Drizzle with lime juice and olive oil, sprinkle with salt and pepper and fold again to combine. Serve at room temperature.

Note: For best taste and texture, do not refrigerate tomatoes or salsa before serving.

MAKES about 2½ cups

Roasted Tomato Salsa

ROASTING IS THE GREAT EQUALIZER that accepts less-than-perfect-looking tomatoes just the way they are. It brings out their sweet and tangy taste, and makes this delicious salsa the perfect way to use up (and appreciate) more challenged-looking garden tomatoes.

1   pound heirloom tomatoes (any variety)

1   jalapeño, stemmed and halved lengthwise

2   tablespoons extra virgin olive oil

2   garlic cloves, minced

½   cup minced red onion

2   tablespoons chopped fresh cilantro

1   tablespoon red wine vinegar

Pinch of sea salt

Freshly ground pepper

Preheat broiler.

Halve tomatoes and cut out blemishes. Place in glass baking dish with jalapeño (with seeds for hot salsa or without seeds for a more mild finished taste). Drizzle with 1 tablespoon olive oil, toss to coat and broil for 10 minutes or until jalapeño is browned. Remove from broiler, remove jalapeño and return tomatoes to broil for 5 minutes longer or until skins start to brown. Remove from heat and set aside to cool.

In skillet over medium heat, sauté garlic and red onion in remaining 1 tablespoon olive oil until soft (2–3 minutes). Remove from heat and place in medium bowl.

Peel and discard skins from pepper, mince and add to bowl with garlic and onion. Peel tomatoes and discard skins but reserve roasting liquid. Chop tomatoes and add to salsa. Stir in cilantro, red wine vinegar and sea salt. Add cooking liquid from roasting, 1 tablespoon at a time to achieve desired consistency. Season to taste with pepper. Serve as is or purée gently with handheld blender for a smoother finish.

MAKES about 1¼ cups

Sarah's Guacamole

MY OLDER DAUGHTER owns all guacamole making in our home. Nobody else is even allowed to think about making it as hers is, of course, the best. It truly couldn't be more simple or delicious, so when she wasn't looking, I wrote down her secret formula so I could share it with you (but please don't tell her I did).

---

4   large avocados, peeled, pitted and chopped

2   garlic cloves, minced

2   tablespoons lime juice

2   tablespoons extra virgin olive oil

¼   teaspoon sea salt

Dash of ground cumin

Dash of cayenne

Place avocados in medium bowl and use fork to gently mash. Add garlic, lime juice, olive oil and salt and fold to combine. Season with cumin and cayenne and serve.

MAKES about 2 cups (depending on size of avocados)

Grilled Pineapple Salsa

I ENJOY THIS SALSA MORE THAN ANY OTHER...that is, when I can keep my family from eating the grilled pineapple on its journey from the grill to the bowl! You'll know what I mean soon enough...

½	pineapple
2	jalapeños, quartered lengthwise and seeded
2	tablespoons extra virgin olive oil, plus more for grilling
2	medium tomatoes, diced
½	cup chopped red onion
1	tablespoon lime juice
2	tablespoons chopped fresh cilantro

Sea salt

Preheat grill to high.

Cut off pineapple's outer skin and cut into thin slices (¼- to ⅓-inch). Rub pineapple slices and jalapeño strips with olive oil and place on grill. Reduce heat to medium and grill 2 minutes per side. Remove from grill and set aside to cool slightly.

In bowl, combine tomatoes and red onion. Chop grilled pineapple and jalapeños and add to bowl. Drizzle with lime juice and 2 tablespoons olive oil. Fold in cilantro and season with sea salt. Toss to combine and serve at room temperature or refrigerate in airtight container.

MAKES about 3 cups (depending on size of pineapple)

Garlic Scape Pesto

THIS SAVORY PESTO IS FAR FROM TRADITIONAL, but can be used in all of your favorite ways — tossed with pasta, mixed with roasted vegetables or spread on crackers or grilled sourdough bread. While garlic scapes are in season, freeze a batch of this pesto for a much welcome taste of summer in the middle of winter.

---

8   garlic scapes, coarsely chopped

½   cup firmly packed fresh cilantro

½   cup extra virgin olive oil, plus more for thinning

½   cup pine nuts

1   teaspoon lemon zest

2   tablespoons lemon juice, plus more for thinning

¼   teaspoon sea salt

Place chopped scapes in food processor and pulse to mince. Add all other pesto ingredients and process until consistent and smooth. Serve or store in airtight container in refrigerator or freezer.

MAKES about 1½ cups

VARIATION
For a smoky twist, grill whole garlic scapes over medium heat for 30 seconds per side before chopping and processing.

Basil Cashew Pesto

I WAS TRYING TO CREATE A PESTO that I could pass off as the real deal, and ended up creating this version made with cashews and lemons that I like even more than the pine nut and Parmesan rendition from my youth. Even my cashew-hating child devours this pesto with delight.

1	large garlic clove, peeled
¾	cup cashews, raw or toasted
2	cups packed fresh basil leaves
2	tablespoons plus 1 teaspoon lemon juice
¼	cup extra virgin olive oil, plus more for thinning
½	teaspoon sea salt

With food processor running, drop in garlic to mince. Turn processor off and add cashews. Process until cashews are finely minced and just starting to become creamy. Add basil, lemon juice, olive oil and sea salt and process until well combined and smooth. For a thinner pesto, add slightly more olive oil. Serve fresh or refrigerate or freeze in airtight containers.

Note: Hardneck garlic is one of my favorite finds at early-summer farmers markets. Its sweet and juicy cloves take this pesto to a whole new level of delicious.

MAKES about 1 cup

Fried Tomatillos with Cilantro Chive Aioli

TOMATILLOS ARE ALMOST MAGICAL, growing like little paper lanterns in the garden. The sweetest fruits come in deep greens and purples, and will not only fill, but will push through their delicate husks. You may know of tomatillos from enjoying them in black bean salad, but wait until you try them fried with this cool and spicy aioli.

6	large tomatillos (about 1 pound)
¼	cup rice milk
1½	cups corn flour
1	teaspoon minced fresh oregano
1	teaspoon minced fresh thyme
¼	teaspoon sea salt
	Freshly ground pepper
	Grapeseed oil for frying

AIOLI

1	jalapeño (optional)
2	tablespoons chopped fresh cilantro
2	tablespoons chopped fresh chives
½	cup grapeseed oil mayonnaise
2	tablespoons lime juice
	Sea salt

Peel back husks from tomatillos and rinse. Slice tomatillos crosswise into ⅓-inch thick slices. Discard stem ends and husks.

Pour the rice milk in a small bowl. In a shallow bowl, combine flour, oregano, thyme, salt and plenty of ground pepper and stir to combine ingredients. Line bowls up next to skillet along with paper towel to absorb excess oil.

Heat large cast iron skillet to medium-high. Pour enough grapeseed oil into skillet to coat bottom of pan. One at a time, submerge tomatillo slices in rice milk, dredge through seasoned flour to coat both sides and place in skillet. Repeat until skillet is full or all tomatillos are used up. Sear each tomatillo slice 1 minute per side or until outsides are crisp and lightly browned. Remove slices from pan and set on paper towel. Repeat to fry all tomatillo slices, adding oil to pan as needed.

If using jalapeño, remove stem and seeds and, with food processor on, drop in pepper to mince. If not using jalapeño, start here: With food processor off, combine cilantro and chives and pulse to mince. Add mayonnaise and lime juice and process gently to combine (so herbs are still visible). Season to taste with salt.

Serve hot tomatillo slices with aioli.

SERVES 4

Raw Chili with Sweet Corn

I'VE JUDGED MY SHARE of chef competitions, but none of the creations stand out as much as the totally raw chili made by the professor from Bridgewater State University who inspired this recipe.

CHILI

4	garlic cloves, peeled
1	jalapeño, stemmed
1	white or yellow onion, quartered
2	red bell peppers, halved and seeded
4	cups coarsely chopped tomatoes (any variety)
2	tablespoons lime juice
3	teaspoons chile powder
1	teaspoon ground cumin
1	teaspoon red wine vinegar
¾	teaspoon sea salt

TOPPINGS

½	avocado, peeled
¼	green bell pepper
¼	cup firmly packed fresh cilantro
2	teaspoons firmly packed oregano leaves
1	scallion, chopped
	Juice of 1 lime
¼	cup extra virgin olive oil
⅛	teaspoon sea salt
2	ears of corn, husked
1	cup cherry tomatoes (mixed varieties and colors), diced
	Extra virgin olive oil for drizzling

Use a food processor or high-powered blender to prepare chili. If using processor, with processor running, drop in garlic and jalapeño (with seeds for hotter chili) and mince. Turn processor off, add onion and red bell peppers and pulse to mince. Add tomatoes, lime juice, chili powder, cumin, vinegar and sea salt and process gently to combine all ingredients. If using high-powered blender, place chili ingredients in container and blend, using tamper to push ingredients down to blade. Transfer chili to serving bowl and set aside.

In clean food processor or blender, combine avocado, green bell pepper, cilantro, oregano, scallion, lime juice, olive oil and sea salt. Process to mince and set aside.

Cut kernels from corn cobs into bowl. Add cherry tomatoes to corn kernels. Holding stripped cobs over separate bowl, scrape cob to release corn milk into bowl. Stir corn milk into chili 1 tablespoon at a time to achieved desired sweetness.

Compose individual servings of chili with a heaping spoonful of corn-tomato mixture and a large dollop of avocado-pepper mixture. Drizzle with olive oil and serve.

SERVES 6

Green Gazpacho

WHEN BLIGHT WIPED OUT MY TOMATOES a few years back, I made salsa out of yellow plums instead. And when the cold and rain kept my tomatoes from ripening, I started making green gazpacho instead of the traditional red. In the end, I always seem to end up thanking Mother Nature for pushing me to think and cook outside the box.

2	garlic cloves, peeled
1	jalapeño, stemmed and seeded
4	large green tomatoes or 16 husked tomatillos, chopped
1	avocado, peeled and pitted
2	tablespoons lime juice
2	tablespoons champagne vinegar
2	tablespoons chopped fresh basil
	Sea salt
2	scallions, chopped
1	lime, cut into wedges

With food processor running, drop in garlic and jalapeño to mince. Turn processor off, add tomatoes and process to chop and combine. Add avocado, lime juice and vinegar. Process until almost smooth. Add basil and pulse to mince and combine. Season to taste with sea salt and serve topped with chopped scallions and a wedge of lime.

SERVES 4

SERVING SUGGESTION
For a zestier finished soup, add an additional jalapeño or replace the jalapeño with a hotter pepper such as a serrano.

Carrot Peach Soup

THERE IS ONE RULE for using the high-powered blender in my home—there always has to be a vegetable in it. This has been a great way to get my kids experimenting with fresh produce. This soup makes it easy to follow the same rule.

1½ cups chopped carrots

¼ small sweet onion, such as Walla Walla or Vidalia

2 cups water

2½ cups peeled and pitted peach wedges

¼ cup coconut milk

1 tablespoon lime juice

1 tablespoon maple syrup

¼ teaspoon ground cinnamon

⅛ teaspoon ground cardamom

Mint leaves for garnish

Place carrots, onion and water in pot over high heat and bring to boil. Reduce heat and simmer 4 minutes or until carrots are barely soft. Add peaches and continue cooking 1 minute longer.

Reserving cooking liquid, use a slotted spoon to transfer solid ingredients to blender. Add coconut milk, lime juice, maple syrup, cinnamon, cardamom and 1 cup reserved cooking liquid and blend until smooth. Serve warm or at room temperature garnished with fresh mint leaves.

SERVES 4

SERVING SUGGESTION
I like to serve this summer soup in espresso cups as an appetizer, in which case this recipe yields 8 servings.

Chopped Salad Cups with Plum Dressing

THIS SALAD IS PRETTY AND SWEET and makes a festive appetizer, too. You can even skip the lettuce cups and serve it as a salsa with salty corn chips or over grilled fish, chicken or zucchini steaks.

---

1   cup peeled, julienned jicama

1   orange bell pepper, diced

1   cup halved red grapes

3   scallions, chopped

2   avocados, peeled, pitted and diced

1   tablespoon lemon juice

2   tablespoons chopped fresh cilantro

8   small Bibb lettuce leaves

¼   cup pistachios, toasted

DRESSING

1   large red plum, peeled, pitted and halved

¼   cup extra virgin olive oil

1   tablespoon red wine vinegar

Pinch of sea salt

In large bowl, combine prepared jicama, bell pepper, grapes and scallions. Place avocado in separate bowl, toss with lemon juice then add to bowl with other vegetables. Fold in cilantro and set aside.

In food processor, mince plum. Scrape down sides. With machine running, pour in olive oil and vinegar and continue processing until liquid. Add sea salt and process to blend.

Pour desired amount of dressing over salad and toss to evenly coat.

Fill each lettuce leaf with a scoop of salad. Chop pistachios, sprinkle over salad and serve.

SERVES 4

VARIATION
This recipe was inspired by the hand-size nasturtium leaves grown at Urban Oaks Organic Farm in New Britain, Connecticut. If you come across similarly large nasturtium leaves, they make a tender and peppery wrap for this sweet salad that will take your cups to a whole new level of yum.

Summer Greens with Edible Flowers and Lemon Champagne Vinaigrette

When it's just too hot for delicate salad greens to grow, I look for some of these delicious alternatives and combine them with the flowers from my herb plants. When the pickings are slim, I use Bibb lettuce or mesclun mix, although it makes for less of an adventure.

VINAIGRETTE

¼ cup extra virgin olive oil

2 tablespoons champagne vinegar

2 teaspoons maple syrup

2 teaspoons lemon juice

½ teaspoon lemon zest

Pinch of sea salt

SALAD

8 cups mixed greens (mizuna, sorrel, baby chard, baby kale, Bibb lettuce, nasturtium leaves, New Zealand spinach, lamb's quarters…)

½ cup edible flowers (nasturtium, chive, sage blossoms, thyme, basil…)

In small bowl, whisk together all vinaigrette ingredients. Place greens in salad bowl. Drizzle with vinaigrette and toss to coat. Arrange edible flowers over the top and serve.

SERVES 6

VARIATIONS

Use vinaigrette as a marinade for artichokes or a dressing for steamed asparagus.

Purslane with Strawberries and Fennel

YOU'RE UNLIKELY TO FIND PURSLANE in your local grocery store. You may, however, have seen it in the cracks of the sidewalk or pulled it from your yard thinking it was a weed. While I try to stick with ingredients that are readily available, this green is such a rich source of omega-3 fatty acids, antioxidants and vitamins A and C that it warranted sharing, just in case you stumble across a clean source.

---

2   cups purslane leaves

1   cup strawberry wedges (or mulberries)

⅓   cup thinly sliced fennel

2   tablespoons thinly sliced red onion

2   tablespoons cold-pressed roasted pistachio oil (or extra virgin olive oil)

1   teaspoon lemon zest

1   tablespoon lemon juice

1   teaspoon maple syrup

Pinch of sea salt

Place purslane leaves, berries, fennel and red onion in bowl and toss to combine. In separate bowl, whisk together pistachio oil, lemon zest, lemon juice, maple syrup and sea salt. Pour dressing over salad, toss to coat and serve.

SERVES 4

Golden Beet and Blackberry Salad

SALADS ARE THE ULTIMATE "dump and stir" recipes and, as a result, end up being my go-to recipes most summer evenings. While it's not often I serve a meal without dark leafy greens, this recipe is the perfect example of how sometimes leaving the greens out better highlights seasonal fresh produce.

1	pound small golden beets of similar size
2	tablespoons chopped chives (save flowers if available)
2	tablespoons extra virgin olive oil
1	tablespoon red wine vinegar
1½	teaspoons maple syrup
2	tablespoons minced fresh mint leaves

Zest of 1 lemon

Sea salt and freshly ground pepper

½	cup blackberries

Preheat oven to 400°F.

Place beets in baking dish, fill with ¼-inch water and cover with foil. Roast 45 minutes or until soft throughout (time will vary depending on size of beets). Remove from heat and set aside to cool. When cool enough to handle, peel or use thumbs to rub away skins, and cut beets into wedges. Place in bowl and add chives.

In small bowl, whisk together olive oil, vinegar, maple syrup, mint and lemon zest. Season to taste with salt and pepper.

Pour three-quarters of dressing over beets and toss to coat. Place berries in separate bowl, add remaining dressing and toss to coat. Transfer beets to serving dish, arrange berries and chive flowers on top and serve.

SERVES 4

Grilled Kohlrabi and Figs with Cipollini Dressing

KOHLRABI IS COOL AND CRUNCHY shaved raw into salads, and tastes totally different when lightly steamed and then grilled. Add figs and cipollini onions, and you have a taste of heaven.

DRESSING

2   medium cipollini onions

¼   cup extra virgin olive oil

1   tablespoon chopped fresh tarragon or thyme

Zest of 1 lemon

2   tablespoons lemon juice

Sea salt and freshly ground pepper

SALAD

2   small kohlrabi, peeled if tough, sliced into ¼-inch rounds

2   red beets (similar size as kohlrabi), peeled and sliced into ¼-inch rounds

1   fennel bulb, halved, cored and cut into ¼-inch wedges

1   teaspoon extra virgin olive oil

1   teaspoon lemon juice

Sea salt and freshly ground pepper

1   tablespoon maple syrup

1   teaspoon balsamic vinegar

6   fresh figs, halved

MAKING DRESSING

Preheat grill to medium-high and grill unpeeled onions until charred on both sides and soft throughout. Remove onions from grill and when cool enough to touch, pinch to remove root ends, peel and discard charred skins. Mince onions and place in small bowl. Add olive oil, chopped herbs, lemon zest and juice, salt and pepper and whisk to combine. Set dressing aside.

GRILLING SALAD

Bring 1 inch of water to boil in medium pot with steaming rack. Place kohlrabi and beets on separate sides of steaming rack. Place fennel on top of kohlrabi. Cover and steam all vegetables until just tender (about 4 minutes). Remove vegetables from steaming rack placing beets in one bowl and kohlrabi and fennel in another. Drizzle with olive oil and lemon juice, sprinkle with salt and pepper and set aside.

In small bowl, whisk together maple syrup and balsamic vinegar. Brush on figs and place cut-side over indirect heat and grill 4–5 minutes or until juices bubble. Place kohlrabi, beets and fennel over direct heat and grill 2–3 minutes per side or until grill lines appear.

Remove vegetables from grill and place back in bowls, still keeping beets separate. Remove figs from grill, being sure to keep cut-side facing up so juices don't spill out, and place on separate plate.

FINISHING SALAD

Compose grilled vegetables on serving dish or individual plates. Drizzle with dressing, arrange with figs and serve warm.

SERVES 4

Garlic Green Beans with Roasted Cherry Tomatoes

I EAT MORE CHERRY TOMATOES AND GREEN BEANS as I work in my garden than I harvest. When I bring enough inside for a meal, I turn to this recipe, which is big on taste and adds a splash of color to any menu.

1½ cups halved cherry tomatoes (mixed varieties)

2 tablespoons extra virgin olive oil

1 teaspoon coarse sea salt

4 large garlic cloves (hardneck if available), thinly sliced

¾ pound green beans, trimmed

½ cup halved and pitted kalamata olives

Freshly ground pepper

Preheat oven to 400°F.

Toss tomatoes with 1 tablespoon olive oil, sprinkle with coarse sea salt and spread in 8 x 8-inch baking dish. Place in oven and roast 30 minutes or until tomatoes start to release their juices.

While tomatoes are roasting, place large skillet over low heat, drizzle with remaining 1 tablespoon olive oil and add garlic. Sauté until garlic is soft and fragrant (about 2 minutes). Transfer garlic to small bowl and set aside.

Increase heat to high, add beans to skillet and sauté until beans turn bright green and start to sear (about 7 minutes). Remove skillet from heat and remove tomatoes from oven. Transfer tomatoes to skillet with beans, being sure to scrape in all of their juices. Add sautéed garlic and olives and fold to combine all ingredients. Season with plenty of pepper and serve hot.

SERVES 4

Hot and Spicy Marinated Cucumbers

MY GARDEN PRODUCES CUCUMBERS long after my creativity for using them has run dry. Farmer Mike at Urban Oaks shared this recipe with me when I was lamenting that I couldn't look at one more cucumber. I've been hooked on these hot and spicy treats ever since, illustrating yet another reason why farmers are so invaluable.

2	medium cucumbers, peeled
1	teaspoon sea salt
1	garlic clove, thinly sliced
½	teaspoon red pepper flakes
¼	cup brown rice vinegar
1	tablespoon toasted sesame oil
1	tablespoon hot pepper sesame oil
1	teaspoon maple syrup
2	tablespoons chopped fresh cilantro
2	tablespoons coarsely chopped dry-roasted peanuts

Halve cucumbers lengthwise and scoop out seeds (a grapefruit spoon works well for this). Slice crosswise into ¼-inch slices and place in bowl. Sprinkle with sea salt, toss to coat and set aside to sit for 2 hours.

Drain water from cucumbers and top with garlic and red pepper flakes. In small pan over medium heat, bring rice vinegar to boil. Remove from heat and pour evenly over cucumber slices. Evenly drizzle sesame oil, hot sesame oil and maple syrup over cucumbers, cover and refrigerate for 1 hour.

Remove cucumbers from refrigerator, toss with cilantro and serve topped with peanuts.

Note: Marinated cucumbers get better with age and can be made well in advance and refrigerated in an airtight container.

SERVES 4

Grilled Avocado with Tomato Peach Salsa

I EAT AVOCADOS STRAIGHT OUT OF THE SHELL with a sprinkle of sea salt or hot sauce. My family thought I was crazy when I threw avocado halves on the grill, until I filled them with this salsa. One taste and they were hooked on eating avocados out of the shells too.

SALSA

- ¾ cup chopped heirloom tomatoes (mixed varieties and colors)
- ¾ cup chopped peaches
- 2 tablespoons minced red onion
- 2 chile peppers of choice (jalapeño, Serrano or other), seeded and minced
- 2 garlic cloves, minced
- ¼ cup chopped fresh cilantro
- Juice of 1 lime
- 1 tablespoon red wine vinegar
- Sea salt and freshly ground pepper

GRILLED AVOCADOS

- 2 avocados
- 1 tablespoon extra virgin olive oil
- Lime juice
- Coarse sea salt and freshly ground pepper
- 2 tablespoons fresh cilantro leaves

Preheat grill to medium-high.

In medium bowl, combine chopped tomatoes, peaches, onion, chile peppers, garlic and cilantro. Fold in lime juice and red wine vinegar, season to taste with sea salt and pepper and set aside.

Halve avocados. Remove and discard pits but do not remove skins. Rub flesh with olive oil and place on grill rack flesh-side down. Grill 5–7 minutes (refrain from moving avocado so you get nice even grill lines). Remove from heat and set aside.

Drizzle avocado quarters with lime juice and a sprinkle of coarse sea salt and pepper. Top with a generous serving of salsa, garnish with cilantro leaves and serve.

SERVES 4

Grilled Zucchini and Pineapple Stack

THERE WAS A TIME WHEN THE VEGETARIAN OPTION at most restaurants was a fairly boring stack of my least favorite vegetables. This recipe is an ode to the countless times it's been my only option. If only I could have called ahead and ordered *this* stack instead.

---

1   pound cipollini onions

Zest and juice of 1 lemon

1   medium zucchini, cut crosswise on an angle into ½-inch slices

1   small pineapple, peeled and cut crosswise into ½-inch slices

Extra virgin olive oil for grilling

½   cup Basil Cashew Pesto (*page 101*)

2   avocados, peeled, pitted and chopped

Aged balsamic vinegar

¼   teaspoon coarse sea salt (variety of choice)

Preheat grill to medium-high.

Grill unpeeled onions until each side is charred and onions are soft throughout (time will vary based on size of onions). Remove onions from grill and when cool enough to touch, pinch to remove root ends, peel and discard charred skins. Place grilled onions in bowl. Add lemon zest and juice and toss to combine.

Rub zucchini and pineapple with olive oil and grill 3–4 minutes on each side or until soft throughout. Remove from grill and set aside.

On individual plates or a serving platter, stack ingredients starting with pineapple, then zucchini, a thin layer of pesto and lastly, onions. Add a second layer as ingredients allow and top each stack with chopped avocado. Finish with a drizzle of balsamic vinegar and a sprinkle of coarse sea salt, and serve.

Note: Ronde de Nice zucchini are a lovely heirloom variety of zucchini sometimes available at farmers markets. When available, cut them crosswise into rounds for this recipe.

SERVES 4

Zucchini and Sweet Corn with Toasted Cumin Seed and Lime

ZUCCHINI IS ONE OF THE SUMMER VEGETABLES that everyone in my family loves. I regularly experiment with new ways to prepare and serve it, but no matter what delicious variations I come up with, we always come back to this recipe.

---

2   zucchini, cut into ½-inch rounds (about 4 cups)

2   ears of corn, husked

1   tablespoon extra virgin olive oil, plus more for grilling

½   teaspoon cumin seed

2   garlic cloves, minced

2   teaspoons lime juice

Coarse sea salt and freshly ground pepper

1   tablespoon chopped fresh cilantro or parsley

Preheat grill to high.

Brush zucchini and corn with olive oil and place on grill. Grill zucchini on each side 3–4 minutes or until lightly charred. Grill corn 2–3 minutes and rotate until all sides are lightly charred. Remove both from grill. Place zucchini in serving dish. Carefully cut corn kernels off cob, add to zucchini and set aside.

In small dry skillet over low heat, toast cumin seed until fragrant. Remove from heat and grind using mortar and pestle and set aside.

In same skillet, sauté garlic in olive oil until lightly browned (about 1 minute). Remove from heat and stir in lime juice, ground toasted cumin, salt and pepper. Pour over zucchini and corn, toss to combine, top with cilantro or parsley and serve.

SERVES 4

Spicy Potato Salad

THE UNDERGROUND DELI IN NEW BRITAIN, CONNECTICUT is a favorite lunch spot for the farmers at Urban Oaks, and is known for its spicy potato salad. One taste and I knew I had to create my own version for my summer repertoire.

1½ pounds Yukon Gold potatoes, unpeeled

1¼ teaspoons sea salt

½ cup minced celery

¼ cup minced red onion

⅓ cup grapeseed oil mayonnaise

½ teaspoon chile powder

¼ teaspoon paprika

1 teaspoon hot pepper sesame oil

Freshly ground pepper

Chop potatoes into 1-inch pieces and place in Dutch oven. Cover with cold water, add 1 teaspoon sea salt and bring to boil. Reduce heat and simmer until potatoes are soft (about 15 minutes). Remove from heat and drain in a colander. Rinse well with cold water to stop cooking and set aside to cool 5–10 minutes. Return potatoes to Dutch oven and add celery and onion.

In small bowl, whisk together mayonnaise, chili powder, paprika, hot sesame oil, remaining ¼ teaspoon sea salt and plenty of pepper. Fold to combine all ingredients and serve at room temperature or refrigerate to chill slightly.

SERVES 4

VARIATION
For even more zip, drizzle 2–3 tablespoons Immune-Boosting Tonic (*page 152*) on the warm drained potatoes before dressing them.

Grilled Sweet Corn with Spicy Rub

WHEN IT COMES TO SWEET CORN, my family is divided. Some of us are purists who like it steamed and simple, and others like to turn up the heat by grilling it with spices. If you're about to make this recipe, you're siding with my half!

---

6   ears of corn

RUB

Juice of 1 lime

1   teaspoon chile paste

½   teaspoon ground coriander

½   teaspoon ground cumin

½   teaspoon paprika

½   teaspoon mustard powder

½   teaspoon sea salt

Preheat grill to medium-high.

Husk corn and place on tray. In small bowl, whisk together all rub ingredients. Brush ears of corn evenly with rub and place side-by-side on grates of grill. Cook 2 minutes per side or until lightly charred all around. Remove corn from grill and serve.

SERVES 6

Roasted Ratatouille

IT WASN'T UNTIL I TASTED THE ASIAN EGGPLANT sold at my local farmers market that I became a fan of eggplant. And once I started roasting it with other vegetables, it was out with the mushy ratatouille I grew up with, and in with this fresh new version where each vegetable stands on its own.

---

2 small Asian eggplants
   (or 1 medium regular)

¼ teaspoon sea salt

1 medium zucchini

1 medium yellow summer
   squash

1 pound tomatoes
   (any variety)

½ red onion, cut into wedges

6 garlic cloves, peeled
   and halved

6 sprigs fresh thyme

2 tablespoons extra virgin
   olive oil

1 teaspoon coarse sea salt

Freshly ground pepper

1 tablespoon balsamic
   vinegar

Preheat oven to 450°F.

Quarter eggplant lengthwise, then cut crosswise into ½-inch slices. Sprinkle with sea salt and place in colander in sink to drain. Use a plate as a weight over eggplant and drain for 30 minutes.

Meanwhile, cut up zucchini and summer squash similarly to eggplant. Cut tomatoes into pieces similar in size to squash pieces.

Arrange, zucchini, summer squash, tomatoes and onion in a single layer in two glass baking dishes. Add drained eggplant, garlic cloves and thyme sprigs and drizzle evenly with olive oil. Sprinkle with sea salt, toss to coat vegetables, and roast for 40 minutes.

Remove from oven, season with plenty of pepper, drizzle with balsamic vinegar and serve.

SERVES 4

SERVING SUGGESTION
Turn this savory dish into a complete meal by serving it tossed with penne pasta or over creamy or grilled polenta.

Pasta with Tomatoes, Basil and Chard

SWISS CHARD IS MY OLDER DAUGHTER'S FAVORITE dark leafy green, making it a requirement in many of our dinners. Thank goodness it grows well in my garden, so I always have plenty available to make this summer version of fast food.

---

1   pound gluten-free penne pasta

3   garlic cloves, peeled

2   cups quartered plum tomatoes

1   cup packed fresh basil leaves

3   tablespoons capers

3   tablespoons extra virgin olive oil

1   small red onion, chopped

2   bunches Swiss chard, chopped (with stems) into bite-size pieces

Generous pinch of sea salt

Pinch of red pepper flakes

Cook penne according to directions on package. Drain into colander, rinse with cool water and set aside.

With food processor running, drop in garlic to mince. Turn processor off and add tomatoes and basil and pulse 2–3 times to chop and combine, but not purée completely (visible chunks of tomatoes and basil leaves are good). Add capers, pulse one final time and set aside.

In Dutch oven over medium heat, sauté onion in olive oil until soft (about 2 minutes). Add chard and fold continuously until wilted. Add pasta and fold to separate clumps and incorporate greens. Fold in tomato-basil mixture, season with salt and pepper flakes and serve.

SERVES 4

Crunchy Quinoa and Cabbage Salad

BLACK AND RED QUINOA ARE SURPRISINGLY DIFFERENT from their ivory counterpart. I love them as much for their nuttier taste and crunchier texture as I do for their beauty. If food is meant to nourish all of our senses, multicolored quinoas definitely deliver.

1	cup tricolor quinoa
2	cups water
¼	teaspoon sea salt, plus more for cooking quinoa
4	cups thinly sliced green cabbage
1	carrot, sliced into thin rounds
5	radishes, thinly sliced
3	scallions, chopped
2	tablespoons mustard seeds
¼	cup extra virgin olive oil
1	tablespoon plus 1 teaspoon ume plum vinegar
1	teaspoon coconut palm sugar

Zest and juice of ½ lemon

Freshly ground pepper

1½	cups halved cherry tomatoes
¼	cup sunflower seeds, toasted
¼	cup chopped fresh flat-leaf parsley or cilantro

Place quinoa in pot or rice cooker with water and pinch of salt. Bring to boil, reduce heat and simmer covered until quinoa is tender and water is absorbed (about 20 minutes). Remove from heat and cool before fluffing.

Place cabbage in large bowl and sprinkle evenly with ¼ teaspoon salt. Firmly massage cabbage until it breaks down and softens (will reduce to about half its original volume). Add carrot, radishes and scallions and toss. Fold in quinoa and set aside.

In small skillet over medium heat, dry-roast mustard seeds until lightly browned and just starting to pop. Remove from heat and whisk in olive oil, ume plum vinegar, coconut sugar, lemon zest and lemon juice. Season to taste with freshly ground pepper.

Pour dressing over salad and toss to coat. Fold in tomatoes, sunflower seeds and parsley and serve.

SERVES 6

Creamy Polenta with Garlic Scapes and Crispy Kale

POLENTA IS ALWAYS AN EASY DINNER OPTION. My family loves it because it's creamy and satisfying and I love it because it's a delicious base for any variety of seasonal vegetables.

---

1 bunch lacinato kale

1 tablespoon extra virgin olive oil, plus more for massaging kale

½ teaspoon fine sea salt

3½ cups vegetable stock

1 cup polenta

6 garlic scapes

Zest of 1 lemon

Coarse sea salt

Preheat grill to high or oven to 400°F.

Remove ends of stalks from kale and place leaves on plate. Massage leaves with olive oil, sprinkle with ¼ teaspoon fine sea salt and grill, or place on parchment-lined baking sheet and roast in the oven. Grill 1–2 minutes per side or roast 10–15 minutes or until kale is dry and crispy. Remove from heat and set aside. When cool, break into 3–4 pieces per leaf.

In medium pot over high heat, bring stock to boil. Stirring continuously, pour in polenta and add remaining ¼ teaspoon fine sea salt. Reduce heat and simmer, stirring occasionally to prevent clumping, until polenta is creamy and thick (about 25 minutes). Remove from heat.

Heat 1 tablespoon olive oil in cast iron skillet over high heat. Cut garlic scapes in half lengthwise to yield long but manageable curls. Place on skillet and sear lightly on each side. Remove from heat when bright green and barely soft.

Transfer polenta to serving dish and top with seared garlic scapes, lemon zest and a pinch of coarse sea salt. Finish with pieces of crispy kale leaves and serve.

Note: Polenta becomes firm when refrigerated, so if you spread leftovers evenly into a baking dish before refrigerating, you can cut out patties to bake or grill for your next meal.

SERVES 4

Millet with Italian Herbs and Cherry Tomatoes

MY FAMILY ENJOYS THIS PREPARATION of millet so much that we eat it year round, changing it just slightly to incorporate seasonal fresh produce. In the spring we add asparagus and chives, in the fall and winter, chopped fennel and beets.

1   cup millet

2   cups vegetable stock or water

Pinch of sea salt

¼   cup coarsely chopped fresh flat-leaf parsley

¼   cup coarsely chopped fresh basil

1   tablespoon coarsely chopped fresh oregano

1   tablespoon extra virgin olive oil

3   dashes ume plum vinegar

1   cup halved cherry tomatoes

Place dry millet in medium saucepan over medium heat and toast until fragrant (about 2 minutes). Add stock or water, and salt. Bring to boil, reduce heat and simmer covered until all liquid is absorbed (about 25 minutes). Remove from heat and set aside to cool slightly (about 5 minutes) before fluffing.

Fluff cooled millet and fold in parsley, basil and oregano. Dress with olive oil and ume plum vinegar and fold to combine. Tomatoes can be folded into grain or served on top.

SERVES 4

VARIATION
When collard greens are harvested in late summer, blanch them whole and use this millet as a stuffing. Add a dollop of pesto or olive tapenade and wrap it up for a satisfying green summer-roll.

Peach, Avocado and Forbidden Rice Nori Rolls

NORI ROLLS ARE LIKE ASIAN BURRITOS—wrapping up all of my favorite ingredients and yielding an entire meal in one easy-to-serve roll. These make a great appetizer or light meal and are one of my favorite foods to pack for a picnic or a day at the beach.

1	cup forbidden black rice
1¾	cups water
	Pinch of sea salt
3	tablespoons sesame seeds
½	teaspoon coarse sea salt
1–2	peaches, pitted and sliced into wedges
1–2	avocados, pitted, peeled and sliced into wedges
3	scallions, cut into 3-inch pieces and sliced length-wise into thin strips
¼	cup pickled sushi ginger
2	teaspoons brown rice syrup
2	teaspoons brown rice vinegar
1	teaspoon hot pepper sesame oil
4	sheets toasted nori
¼	cup tamari

Place rice in pot or rice cooker with water and salt. Bring to boil, reduce heat and simmer covered until rice is tender and water is absorbed (about 30 minutes). Remove from heat and set aside to cool slightly.

In dry skillet over medium heat, pan-roast sesame seeds until lightly browned and fragrant. Remove from heat and transfer seeds to mortar. Add sea salt and use pestle to grind seeds and salt together until half the seeds are ground. Place next to work surface along with peaches, avocados, scallions and sushi ginger.

Drizzle syrup, vinegar and sesame oil over rice, toss to combine and add to line-up with other prepared ingredients.

Place a sheet of nori, shiny side down, on work surface or bamboo rolling mat, with a short side facing you. Press a thin layer of rice over the bottom third of the nori sheet (the side closer to you). Place peaches, avocados, scallions and ginger in a long thin strip across the middle of the rice. Sprinkle on sesame-salt mixture, then carefully fold the end of nori over the rice and continue rolling away from you to form a log. Moisten the edge with water to seal, and let roll sit 2–3 minutes for nori to soften. Cut crosswise into ½-inch pieces, arrange on serving dish and repeat to use up ingredients. Serve with tamari on the side for dipping.

SERVES 4

VARIATION
Substitute mango when peaches are out of season.

Sprouted Quinoa Confetti Salad

SPROUTING BRINGS GRAINS TO THE PEAK POINT of germination where their nutrients are more accessible and the grains themselves are easier to digest. Plan in advance to leave enough time for sprouting and be careful not to let grains go too long as they will start to lose their health benefits.

1	cup quinoa
2	cups water
1	cup halved cherry tomatoes
1	cup cooked chickpeas
½	orange bell pepper, diced
½	cup pitted and halved kalamata olives
½	cup chopped scallions
½	cup finely chopped fennel
¼	cup chopped fresh basil
2	tablespoons capers
2	tablespoons extra virgin olive oil
1	tablespoon red wine vinegar

Sea salt and freshly ground pepper

SPROUTING QUINOA

Place quinoa in bowl with water and soak 6 hours or overnight. Drain soaking water and rinse quinoa in fine-mesh strainer. Place strainer with quinoa over bowl on counter, cover with clean kitchen towel and set aside to sprout. Rinse quinoa well 3–4 times a day and leave covered on counter until sprouted (18–24 hours).

PREPARING SALAD

In large bowl, combine tomatoes, chickpeas, bell pepper, olives, scallions, fennel, basil and capers. Fold in sprouted quinoa and continue folding to evenly distribute all ingredients. Drizzle with olive oil and vinegar and toss to combine. Season to taste with salt and pepper and serve.

SERVES 6

Sprouted Chickpea Salad

SPROUTED LEGUMES ARE EASY TO MAKE and worth the effort to benefit from their improved nutritional value. Sprouting makes the nutrients in legumes easier to assimilate, easier to digest and even increases their vitamin content. You can always make this recipe with cooked chickpeas, but if you've never sprouted chickpeas before, this is the perfect opportunity to give it a try.

½ cup dried chickpeas (yields 1½ cups sprouted)

2 cups water

1 cup halved cherry tomatoes

½ cup pitted and halved kalamata olives

¼ cup chopped red onion

1 tablespoon chopped fresh flat-leaf parsley

1 tablespoon chopped fresh basil

1 medium cucumber, peeled

3 tablespoons extra virgin olive oil

1 garlic clove, peeled

3 sun-dried tomatoes in oil, drained and minced

Zest and juice of 1 lemon

½ teaspoon coarse sea salt

Freshly ground pepper

SPROUTING CHICKPEAS

Place chickpeas in bowl with water and soak 6 hours or overnight. Drain soaking water and rinse chickpeas in wire-mesh strainer. Place strainer over bowl on counter, cover with clean kitchen towel and set aside to sprout. Rinse beans well 3–4 times a day and leave covered on counter until sprouted (2–3 days).

PREPARING SALAD

In large bowl, combine tomatoes, olives, onion, parsley and basil. Halve cucumber, scoop out and discard seeds, chop and add to bowl with vegetables. Rinse sprouted chickpeas thoroughly and fold into vegetable mixture.

In small bowl, whisk together olive oil, garlic, sun-dried tomatoes, lemon juice and lemon zest. Drizzle dressing over salad, sprinkle with coarse sea salt and season to taste with pepper. Toss to combine all ingredients and serve.

Salad can be stored in airtight container for up to 4 days.

SERVES 6

Roasted Tomatoes, Cipollinis and White Beans on Grilled Bread

EVERY FRIDAY, SWEET SAGE BAKERY DELIVERS freshly baked sourdough breads to Urban Oaks just before opening. The grains are locally grown and milled, and the sourdough is warm when I arrive. It's far too delectable to be relegated to the side of the meal, so I build main courses, like this one, around it.

4	cups heirloom tomatoes (any variety)
2	cups small cipollini onions, peeled
3	tablespoons extra virgin olive oil, plus more for grilling bread
3	garlic cloves, peeled
1	tablespoon minced fresh sage
1	cup cooked white beans (navy, great northern or cannellini)
½	cup fresh basil leaves

Sea salt and freshly ground pepper

6	slices sourdough or gluten-free bread

Aged balsamic vinegar

Preheat oven to 400°F.

Chop tomatoes into similar-size chunks (about 1½ inches) and place in baking dish. Add cipollini onions, toss with 2 tablespoons olive oil and roast 35 minutes or until tomatoes are soft and juicy and onions are soft throughout. Remove from oven and set aside.

Preheat grill to high.

Mince 2 garlic cloves. In cast iron skillet over low heat, sauté garlic in remaining 1 tablespoon olive oil until soft (about 2 minutes). Add sage and sauté a minute longer. Drain beans well, add to skillet and sauté to heat through. Add roasted tomatoes and onions and scrape baking dish to add in any extra juices. Fold in basil and season to taste with salt and pepper. Turn off heat and set aside.

Brush both sides of bread slices with olive oil. Halve remaining garlic clove and rub cut-sides of garlic generously over both sides of bread. Grill bread 1 minute on each side or until crispy with seared grill lines on the outside and soft on the inside.

Top grilled bread with tomato-onion mixture, drizzle with balsamic vinegar and serve.

SERVES 4

Black Lentil Salad with Curry Vinaigrette

I CRAVE THIS COMBINATION of black lentils and curry vinaigrette all year long. As a result, I adapt this recipe for each season, serving it with cucumbers and tomatoes in summer, roasted winter squash and Brussels sprouts in fall and winter, and sautéed ramps in spring.

1   cup black lentils

3   cups water

1   thumb-size piece kombu

Pinch of sea salt

½   cup chopped red onion

1   cup chopped cucumber

1   cup chopped tomato

2   jalapeños (or other chile pepper of choice), seeded and minced

½   cup chopped fresh cilantro

VINAIGRETTE

4   tablespoons extra virgin olive oil

2   tablespoons red wine vinegar

3   garlic cloves, minced

1   teaspoon curry powder

Sea salt and freshly ground pepper

Rinse lentils and sort to clean. Place in medium pot with water, kombu and sea salt. Bring to boil, reduce heat to low and simmer covered until just tender (about 20 minutes). Remove from heat, drain any remaining water and set aside to cool slightly.

In large bowl, combine red onion, cucumber, tomato, jalapeños and cilantro. Remove and discard kombu, fold in lentils and set aside.

In small bowl, whisk together olive oil, red wine vinegar, garlic and curry. Season to taste with sea salt and pepper and pour over lentil salad. Fold to coat all ingredients and serve.

SERVES 6

Black Bean Mango Tacos

TACOS ARE MY ANSWER to "make your own dinner," and leftovers meet their demise when it's taco night at my house. I'll put just about anything out for my family to use as filling for their tacos, which can inspire many new combinations, like this one.

8   corn taco shells

2   tablespoons extra virgin olive oil

2   garlic cloves, minced

2   jalapeños, seeded and minced

¼   cup chopped red onion

2   cups cooked black beans

½   teaspoon chile powder

½   teaspoon ground cumin

⅛   teaspoon sea salt

2   tablespoons lime juice

1   large mango, peeled, pitted and diced

2   tablespoons chopped fresh cilantro

Freshly ground pepper

1   cup chopped tomatoes

2   avocados, peeled, pitted and chopped

Preheat oven to 350°F.

Spread taco shells on baking sheet and toast 5 minutes. Remove from heat and set aside.

In cast iron skillet over medium heat, sauté garlic, jalapeños and onion in 1 tablespoon olive oil until soft (about 3 minutes). Add black beans, increase heat to high and sauté 2 minutes longer. Stir in chili powder, cumin, salt and lime juice and sauté 1 minute longer to allow flavors to blend before removing from heat.

In separate bowl, toss together mango and cilantro, and season with plenty of ground pepper.

Assemble tacos with black bean mixture on the bottom, mango next, chopped tomatoes and chopped avocado over the top, and serve.

SERVES 4 (two tacos each)

Shiitake Mushroom Bean Burgers

SUMMER BARBECUES ARE A CINCH…until there are guests who just aren't satisfied unless there's a burger. For those times, when a grilled portobello mushroom cap just won't do, here's a burger that's grillworthy.

1½ cups cooked cannellini or great northern beans

1 tablespoon extra virgin olive oil

3 garlic cloves, minced

1 small red onion, chopped

½ cup thinly sliced shiitake mushroom caps

1½ teaspoons minced fresh rosemary

1 tablespoon chopped fresh oregano

3 tablespoons minced sun-dried tomatoes

¼–½ teaspoon sea salt

Freshly ground pepper

1 tablespoon chopped fresh flat-leaf parsley

3 tablespoons gluten-free bread or rice crumbs

Extra virgin olive oil for grilling or sautéing

Place beans in processor and pulse to partially mash (leaving half of beans still showing).

Heat oil in large skillet over medium heat. Add garlic and onion and sauté 2 minutes. Add shiitakes and sauté until soft and lightly browned (about 2 minutes longer). Add rosemary, oregano and sun-dried tomatoes and sauté 2 minutes longer. Transfer mixture to food processor with beans and pulse to combine ingredients. Season to taste with salt and plenty of pepper and pulse one more time.

Transfer bean mixture to a bowl and fold in parsley and breadcrumbs. Form into six patties 2½ inches across and ¾-inch thick and set aside for 5 minutes for patties to firm. Burgers can be grilled (my preferred method), sautéed or baked.

GRILL

3 minutes per side over medium-high heat on well-oiled grill (oil again when flipping burgers).

SAUTÉ

3 minutes per side in cast iron skillet over medium-high heat with just enough olive oil to thinly cover bottom of skillet.

BAKE

15 minutes per side in 400°F oven on parchment-lined baking sheet.

Burgers will be crispy on the outside and soft on the inside. Serve warm or bring to room temperature and then wrap individually to freeze for later use.

MAKES 6 burgers

Raspberry Rhubarb Cobbler

WHAT DESSERT IS EASIER TO MAKE THAN COBBLER? None. And when it comes right down to it, none is as appreciated as cobbler made from the berries we picked that day!

FILLING

4   cups sliced rhubarb
    (½-inch slices)

2   cups raspberries

1   tablespoon arrowroot

Pinch of ground cloves

Pinch of sea salt

½   cup maple syrup

TOPPING

1   cup pecans

½   cup gluten-free rolled oats

¼   cup coconut palm sugar

Pinch of sea salt

¼   cup virgin coconut oil,
    melted

Preheat oven to 400°F.

Place rhubarb and raspberries in large bowl and sprinkle with arrowroot, cloves and sea salt. Pour on maple syrup and fold to combine ingredients and dissolved powder in syrup. Pour into 8 x 8-inch baking dish (or similar size) and set aside.

In food processor, combine pecans, oats, sugar and salt and process until mixture resembles coarse meal. Add coconut oil and process until evenly moist. Crumble over top of rhubarb mixture and bake 20 minutes, or until fruit bubble and top is lightly browned.

Remove from oven and cool 5 minutes before serving.

SERVES 6

Watermelon Ice with Coconut Milk

I COMBINED MY FAMILY'S two most refreshing summer desserts into one with this uber-refreshing ice cream. If you don't have watermelon on hand, you'll be equally happy substituting peaches or mango.

---

4 cups seeded, cubed watermelon

¼ cup whole coconut milk

¼ cup maple syrup

¼ lime (with skin if using high-powered blender and without for regular kitchen blender)

Pinch of ground nutmeg

Place watermelon cubes in airtight container and freeze until firm.

In blender, combine frozen watermelon with coconut milk, maple syrup, lime and nutmeg. Cover and blend on high for 30 seconds or until consistent and smooth, using tamper to push ingredients down to blade to be blended. Serve immediately.

Note: Recipe can be made in advance and frozen for up to 2 hours before serving. To prevent it from becoming icy, remove from freezer every hour, fold to mash and maintain smooth texture and return to freezer.

MAKES about 2 cups

SERVING SUGGESTIONS
Serve with fresh berries or mint leaves to garnish, try a scoop over a brownie or waffle, or dress it up with a lemon cookie or wafer.

Cantaloupe Ginger Lime Sorbet

A LITTLE ADVANCED PLANNING IS ALL IT TAKES to make your own delicious sorbet. I keep cut-up melon in my freezer all summer so that I'm always prepared for those spontaneous sorbet cravings.

4	cups cubed cantaloupe
1	1-inch piece fresh ginger, peeled and thinly sliced
¼	cup maple syrup
¼	lime (with skin if using high-powered blender and without for regular kitchen blender)
1	tablespoon minced candied ginger

Place cantaloupe cubes in airtight container and freeze until firm.

In blender, combine frozen melon with fresh ginger, maple syrup and lime. Cover and blend on high for 30 seconds or until consistent and smooth, using tamper to push ingredients down to blade to be blended. Serve immediately topped with candied ginger.

Note: Sorbet can be made in advance and frozen for up to 2 hours before serving. To prevent it from becoming icy, remove from freezer every hour, fold to mash and maintain smooth texture and return to freezer.

MAKES about 2 cups

Dark Chocolate and Hot Pepper Covered Ground Cherries

ALSO KNOWN AS HUSK TOMATOES, ground cherries grow like tiny tomatillos with thin brown protective shells. The berries fall to the ground when they're ready to harvest, and taste like a cross between a strawberry and a cherry tomato.

---

1   cup ground cherries with husks

½   cup gluten-free dark chocolate chunks

½   teaspoon virgin coconut oil

Dash of ground cinnamon

Pinch of ground chile powder

1   chile pepper (variety and of choice), stemmed and seeded

Carefully pull back husks from ground cherries but leave them attached so they look like they have petals or wings. Rinse fruit under water, one at a time, being careful not to get husks wet. Allow fruit to dry completely.

Line plate with parchment paper.

In small pot over low heat, melt chocolate and coconut oil until smooth. Remove from heat and stir in cinnamon and chile powder. Cut chile pepper in half and add to melted chocolate. Using the back of a spoon (or garlic press), press pepper to partially crush and release juices into chocolate and stir to infuse chocolate with pepper juice. Remove pepper pieces from chocolate and discard (or eat if you dare).

Holding cherries by their husks, dip into chocolate to cover fruit. When chocolate stops dripping, place on parchment paper to set. If chocolate starts to harden before all cherries are dipped, return pot to low heat and stir until liquid.

Set aside or refrigerate to allow chocolate to harden and serve.

MAKES about 20 pieces

VARIATIONS
This recipe is equally delicious made with clementine wedges in winter.

Coconut Cacao Energy Bars

IF I DIDN'T CREATE MY OWN ENERGY BAR RECIPES, I would likely go broke on nutrition bars. I just have to have something in me before my morning run and these homemade energy bars (and the NoNo Bars on *page 272)* are my fuel of choice. I even wrap them up in parchment paper to take on the road when I'm riding my bike.

3   cups pitted large Medjool dates

3   tablespoons virgin coconut oil

¾   cup cacao beans or nibs

¾   cup unsweetened dried shredded coconut

⅛   teaspoon ground cinnamon

2   pinches of coarse sea salt

Place dates in bowl, cover with hot water and set aside to soften. Melt coconut oil in small pan over low heat. Grind cacao beans in coffee grinder to yield a coarse flour with a few small chunks.

In large bowl, combine coconut, cinnamon and salt. Drain dates and press to remove excess liquid. Add to coconut mixture along wtih oil and nibs and mashtogether all ingredients.

Rinse and drain an 8 x 8-inch glass baking dish and press batter into dish. Cover and refrigerate for at least 30 minutes to set. When ready to serve, remove from refrigerator, cut into 20 bars (about 1 x 2 inches each) and serve.

MAKES 20 bars

Dark Chocolate Chunk Cookies

MAY YOUR SEARCH FOR the perfect vegan, gluten-free chocolate chip cookie end here!

DRY INGREDIENTS

1½ cups almond flour/meal

½ cup sweet white sorghum flour

½ cup tapioca flour

1 teaspoon baking soda

1 teaspoon sea salt

WET INGREDIENTS

½ cup maple syrup

¼ cup virgin coconut oil, melted

¼ cup applesauce

1½ teaspoons vanilla extract

½ cup gluten-free dark chocolate chunks

½ teaspoon coarse sea salt (optional)

Place all dry ingredients in large bowl and whisk to combine well and eliminate lumps. In separate small bowl, whisk together all wet ingredients. Pour wet ingredients into dry and stir to form consistent dough. Fold in chocolate chunks, cover with plastic wrap or parchment paper (so not exposed to air) and refrigerate 1 hour.

Preheat oven to 350°F. Line 2 baking sheets with parchment paper.

Remove dough from refrigerator. Scoop dough out in heaping teaspoons and place 2–3 inches apart on baking sheets. Bake for 8 minutes or until cookies are lightly browned. Remove from oven and top each cookie with a few grains of sea salt if desired. Cool on rack before serving.

Note: Sorghum, a cereal grass traditionally grown in Africa, is ground into a light, gluten-free flour available in most natural foods stores.

MAKES 2 dozen

FALL

Inside, my kitchen overflows with produce waiting to be preserved. Herbs and peppers hang on the beams to dry, the dehydrator hums around the clock, and the tangy smell of lacto-fermenting foods fills the air. Outside, leaves in shades of red, gold and yellow cover the trees and float gently to the ground. Plants dry out slowly, but continue to produce. Kale and collard greens grow more hardy and sweet, reaching up to take in the sun as the vines of the winter squash stretch across the garden. The husk tomatoes drop to the ground calling for me to collect them. And the root vegetables show off their greens, tempting me to pull them from the earth. Fall rushes by so quickly. Perhaps the pace is set by the return to the school schedule, the race to preserve everything, or the ever-looming threat of frost and snow. Every day I take in the blanket of foliage and the crunching of leaves under foot, and I breathe in the fresh air, suddenly much cleaner as a result of the cool temperature. The need to close up shop for the season hangs over me like having to say goodbye to a dear friend. When winter arrives, I will be prepared and grateful for the rest. Until then, I remain thankful for the gifts of Mother Nature and I celebrate the harvest.

CONTENTS

A Strong Immune System

With fall's bounty of fresh produce, remaining healthy throughout the season should be easy, but often it can be a struggle. The faster pace and added stresses of back-to-work and back-to-school necessitate an increase in my efforts to strengthen my immune system. Add to that more time indoors, greater exposure to germs, seasonal allergens like ragweed and mold, and the upcoming cold and flu season, and I turn my focus to making my family and myself as strong as possible.

DIET AND THE IMMUNE SYSTEM

Eating clean means nourishing ourselves with a variety of minimally processed vegetables, fruits, whole grains, legumes, nuts and seeds, as close to the source as possible. The more we fill our plates with in-season, locally grown produce, the more we benefit from the nutrition provided by Mother Nature, and the more easily we can maintain balance with our environment. Here's what that looks like in practice during the fall.

DECREASE INFLAMMATION

Following a diet rich in anti-inflammatory foods not only supports the immune system but also helps prevent many chronic diseases. These are important foods, but it's not necessary to make them the entirety of your diet. Clean foods that don't fall into the anti-inflammatory category can still offer good nutrition (e.g., whole grains). Knowing the healing value of foods allows us to make healthy choices and use a variety of foods to achieve overall health and well-being. Anti-inflammatory foods are beneficial year-round, not only by supporting the immune system, but by decreasing risk of heart disease, cancer, Alzheimer's, diabetes, chronic pain and a host of autoimmune diseases.

We naturally crave more warming cooked foods as the weather gets colder, but a healthy dose of raw foods is also important for reducing inflammation. Cooking can make some nutrients more bioavailable, but including raw foods is also important as more delicate, heat sensitive nutrients are preserved.

Carotenoid-rich, high-antioxidant foods are important for reducing inflammation. You'll know these foods by their colorful pigmentation—dark leafy greens and cruciferous vegetables (such as kale, Brussels sprouts and broccoli), plus tomatoes, sweet potatoes, carrots, bell peppers, winter squashes and berries.

Culinary herbs, spices and roots offer a host of health benefits in addition to their significant anti-inflammatory properties. Choose from cinnamon, curry, ginger, mint, oregano, parsley, rosemary and sage.

Load up on these heavy-hitters: onions and chile peppers for the antioxidant quercetin, which has anti-inflammatory and antihistamine properties; turmeric for its rich source of cancer-fighting curcumin; and garlic, for the antibacterial, anticancer and heart-healthy allicin it forms when crushed or chopped and allowed to sit for 5–10 minutes.

While good fats are key to reducing inflammation, a balance of omega-3 and omega-6 fatty acids is the goal. Good fats like those from extra virgin olive oil, virgin coconut oil, ghee (clarified butter), avocados and avocado oil should be combined with sources of omega-3 fats such as nuts and seeds and their oils (flax, hemp, chia, walnut and sesame), cold-water fish and fish oil.

Reducing consumption of unhealthy omega-6 fats is critical for decreasing inflammation. Refined corn oil, safflower oil, sunflower oil, canola oil, cottonseed oil, hydrogenated and partially hydrogenated fats should be avoided. Other key inflammatory foods to reduce or eliminate include sugar, dairy, conventional and processed meat products, fried foods and refined grains.

Sea vegetables offer a rich source of alkalinizing minerals and anti-inflammatory properties. Dried kombu can be added to cooking grains and legumes to infuse them with minerals and make them less inflammatory. Other sea vegetables to include are arame, nori and wakame.

Finally, it would be out of character if I failed to mention dark chocolate. Both dark chocolate and green tea are heart-healthy and anti-inflammatory when consumed in moderation (that's the hard part for me).

Identifying foods that cause inflammation empowers me even more to make the choices to support reducing inflammation and boosting immune strength, but food is not the only way we have of decreasing inflammation. While we can't always reduce the stress in our lives, we can change our body's response to it by practicing mindfulness. The more stress we have, the more our "fight or flight" response is activated, and the more the body responds with inflammation. Meditation, yoga and tai chi relieve the weight of stressful situations and reduce the inflammatory response as a result.

INCORPORATE ROOTS AND HERBS

Roots and herbs can help us counter the negative effects of stress, stimulate the immune system and increase resistance to bacteria and viruses. Herbs can be taken as tinctures or steeped in hot water for 2–3 hours to make medicinal teas. Some, such as maca root, can even be purchased as powder that can be used as a nutritive sweetener. Check with your physician, naturopath or herbalist to understand which herbs are best suited for you: ashwaghandha root, astragulus root, echinacea, elderberry, ginseng, holy basil leaf, licorice root, maca root, milky oats, nettles, rosehips and schisandra.

HEAL WITH MUSHROOMS

Mushrooms also offer a wealth of health benefits. Even the most humble white button mushroom is an excellent source of antioxidants, but there are a variety of mushrooms to choose from in order to take advantage of their anti-inflammatory, antiviral, antibacterial, and cholesterol and blood pressure regulating properties. Some of my favorite healing mushrooms are reishi, shiitake and maitake.

DIY IMMUNE-BOOSTING TONICS

There are many ways to take advantage of the healing and medicinal properties of food without purchasing premade tonics. My recipes use food as medicine, which makes supporting good health easy and delicious, but I also depend on a few homemade tonics.

Start with a simple tonic made by steeping dried mushrooms or herbs in hot water for a minimum of 20 minutes, or by gently simmering roots for 30 minutes or longer. The longer the tonic steeps, the more powerful the medicine. When done, strain to remove solids and store the tonic for later use. Even if I don't have time to prepare a tonic, I add a piece of dried astragulus root or a crumbled dried shiitake mushroom to cooking grains, soups and legumes to increase the healing properties of my foods.

Tonics also include warm and soothing drinks, such as hot chocolate! Who can pass up hot cocoa made from coconut or almond milk, raw cacao, local raw honey, grated fresh ginger and nutmeg? Increase the heat and the healing power by adding crushed chile pepper and you've got antioxidant-rich, immune-supporting heaven in a mug.

Vinegar-based tonics have long been used for deep immune support and combine a variety of roots and herbs to help treat everything from the basic cold and congestion to ear infections and flu. As with many folk medicines, this recipe was passed on to me by a wise woman, the founder of The Institute of Sustainable Nutrition. I have shared it with my family and friends, and now you can share it with yours. I make my tonic in the fall when the plants above ground have started to die back, sending their nutrients down into the roots. I make a big batch so that I can gift it at the holidays and still have plenty on hand to get though the rest of the year.

IMMUNE-BOOSTING TONIC

I take 1 tablespoon of immune-boosting tonic each day during the cold and flu season for maintenance. If I feel something coming on, I add an extra dose or two throughout the day. This tonic is quite strong, so mix it with juice or tea (it's especially good in vanilla tea). You can also incorporate it into your cooking by adding it to salad dressings, marinades, soups, salsas, pickles.... Oh, so many possibilities!

½ cup grated fresh ginger
½ cup grated fresh horseradish root
1 cup chopped onion
10 garlic cloves, crushed
3 tablespoons grated fresh turmeric root
1 fresh cayenne chile pepper, minced
1 lemon, zest and juice
3 sprigs fresh rosemary
3 slices dried astragalus root
Organic apple cider vinegar
Local raw honey

Place ginger, horseradish, onion, garlic, turmeric, cayenne, lemon zest and lemon juice in a nonreactive bowl (glass or ceramic). Use your hands to mix ingredients together well and then pack firmly into a 1-quart mason jar. Wedge rosemary and astragalus down along sides of jar so they are well below the top layer of ingredients. Pour in enough apple cider vinegar to cover ingredients. Place a sheet of parchment paper over the top of the jar and screw on lid. Shake jar and set aside in cool dry place out of direct sunlight. Let cider sit for 1 month, but be sure to shake it daily (I call that "giving it the love").

Drape a piece of cheesecloth over a large bowl and empty contents of jar into it. Pull up sides of cloth, twist top to close and squeeze as much juice as possible into the bowl. Discard solids and taste cider. Add honey, a little at a time, to achieve desired taste and return to jar.

Note: Please wear gloves (especially when mincing the chiles) and work in a well-ventilated space to avoid overwhelming horseradish fumes.

Preserving The Harvest

You don't need to have your own garden to benefit from preserving the harvest. Perhaps your weekly CSA share had more greens in it than you knew what to do with, or you got a steal on past-prime tomatoes at the farm. Maybe the herbs on the windowsill are outgrowing their pots, or neighbors gave you a bag of produce from their garden. Preserving is a healthful solution that's easy, safe, economical and delicious.

While I have canning pots and racks in the basement, I admit that they've not seen the light of day in years. I love pickled fiddleheads, dilly beans, beets and many other canned goods, but for the sake of this book, I'm going to stick with preserving methods that do not cook ingredients first, and that require less time and effort.

DRYING
Herbs and chile peppers

It doesn't get easier than this. If you buy more fresh herbs than you can use, try drying them (instead of leaving them in the refrigerator to rot).

Wash and dry them, tie the ends together (or use a rubber band) and hang them upside down. Ideally, you want to hang them in a cool dry place out of direct sunlight. I often hang mine on the knobs of my kitchen cabinets. Different herbs take different amounts of time to dry. In my home, as soon as someone opens a cabinet and complains about herbs crumbling onto the counter, I figure they're done (this is very high tech, I know).

Chile peppers can be dried similarly, but have to be strung. I keep a needle and thread in the kitchen for this and string the peppers through their stems, then hang them horizontally so the peppers aren't touching. Sunlight is helpful for drying peppers, so you can use the window for them.

With both herbs and peppers, make sure you've washed and dried everything thoroughly before bunching or stringing them to prevent mold from growing. Once dry, keep the herbs and peppers whole or crumbled, transfer into glass jars, seal and store.

DEHYDRATING
Most vegetables, herbs, berries and fruit

Hanging to dry is the greenest (and prettiest) method of preserving. However, dehydrating speeds up the drying process significantly; can be done in a dehydrator or oven that can be heated to 110°F; and makes it possible to preserve a greater variety of items. Regardless of which appliance you use, there are a few guidelines.

1. Wash and dry produce thoroughly.

2. Cut produce into similar-size pieces.

3. Dehydrate until food is completely dry.

4. Store dehydrated produce in glass containers.

5. If condensation becomes apparent in the container within the first week after dehydrating, remove from jar and dehydrate further.

Air circulation facilitates even dehydration. Dehydrators are designed to have excellent air circulation, but if using an oven with solid baking sheets, be extra careful that items are not touching since air circulation is more limited and overlapping leaves can trap moisture. Herbs laid in a single layer on a baking sheet and dried in an oven will take 2–4 hours and even less time in a dehydrator.

Some of my favorite items to dehydrate are tomatoes, chile peppers, onions, mushrooms, leeks, apple slices, mango slices and sprouted nuts and seeds. I'm also partial to making kale chips *(page 168)*, a variety of fruit leathers *(page 208)* and even banana chips (especially loved by the dog). Dehydrators are also particularly good (and fun) for making raw, gluten-free and sprouted crackers and breads.

LACTO-FERMENTING
Most vegetables

The first time I made my own sauerkraut, I was afraid to eat it. For starters, I never even liked sauerkraut. I was in it for the health benefits, not the taste. Knowing little about the process at the time, I assumed the chances were good that I had done something wrong. Afterall, it had just sat on my counter for two weeks! Not only did I live to write about it, but it was perfectly safe and delicious. The taste was like no kraut I had ever had before. This was NOT the mysterious bottle that lived in the back of our refrigerator when I was a child. I have been making lacto-fermented foods ever since.

Lacto-fermentation uses microorganisms to transform food and yields the following benefits:

Greater nutritional value, as the fermentation processes generates B vitamins and vitamin K.

Easier digestibility from nutrients being made more bioavailable.

Increased beneficial bacteria and probiotics necessary for healthy bodily function, nutrient absorption and immune health.

Improved taste.

Healthy, safe and preserved.

There are a variety of methods that can be used to lacto-ferment produce. I've provided recipes for three approaches to get you started. The first, making sauerkraut, involves massaging the cabbage to break down the cell walls, extracting the water and fermenting the cabbage in its own brine *(page 165)*. The second method I use to make kimchi *(page 166)*. Here, the vegetables are soaked in a prepared brine to break down the cell walls. They're then drained, combined with spices and fermented (also) in their own brine. And finally, a lacto-fermentation that involves simply soaking vegetables with herbs and spices in prepared brine as in the Pretty in Pink Pickled Radishes *(page 41)*.

As long as the fermenting vegetables remain below the level of brine (a weight such as a small bottle makes this easy), they are safe. Vegetables develop different beneficial bacteria throughout the lacto-fermentation processes. Taste each day to discover the degree of fermentation you like best. Any vegetables that are above the level of brine and are exposed to air can grow mold. If that happens, discard those pieces and enjoy the vegetables that were safely fermenting in the brine. When your vegetables reach the point of sourness and crispiness you like best, remove the weight, seal the jar and transfer to the refrigerator to slow down the fermentation.

Lacto-fermenting your own sauerkraut yields a very different product than what you buy in the store. If purchasing fermented goods, always read the ingredients. If it is made with vinegar as opposed to salt, it is pickled and not fermented. While there are a few artisanal lacto-fermented krauts available, hermetically sealing containers often involves high heat that in turn kills living enzymes. In the end, the effort to make your own is minimal compared to the nutritional value it gives back.

I always keep a rotating supply of fermented foods on hand. I may have a bottle of kraut fermenting on the counter while I'm working on a bottle of kimchi or radishes in the refrigerator. When those are done and the kraut moves to the refrigerator, it's anybody's guess what will be put up to ferment next! Perhaps carrots, daikon, ginger, turmeric, garlic scapes, ramps, green tomatoes, cucumbers…. Everything is fair game.

FREEZING

I keep a variety of frozen fruits and vegetables in my freezer at all times just to make life easier. Freezing allows produce to retain much of its nutritional value and there's nothing like taking out a bag of frozen blueberries picked fresh in the summer and adding them to hot cereal in the middle of winter. Yum!

Fruits and vegetables can become soft when thawed, so don't expect the fresh crisp texture of vine-picked summer produce. That said, frozen vegetables are perfect to add to winter soups, stews and casseroles, and fruits can be used in smoothies, crisps, hot cereals or eaten as is (my youngest daughter loves to snack on frozen blueberries and even peas—just not together).

The best way to freeze produce is to wash and dry it thoroughly. Use parchment paper to line a plate or baking sheet that fits in your freezer. Spread vegetables or fruit in a single layer and place in freezer until frozen (items will be firm and solid). Remove from freezer, transfer to an airtight container and return to freezer until ready to use.

CLOSING UP SHOP

Unless you have a greenhouse or a hoop house to extend the growing season, the period of vegetable nirvana, otherwise known as the fall harvest, is coming to an end. Before heading inside, I sprinkle remaining composted material on my gardens and dig trenches in which to plant my garlic.

It's believed by farmers that garlic grows best when planted under the full moon, which works in my favor. Usually I am so late getting my garlic into the ground that I could literally be outside, planting under the full moon on one of the final evenings before the first frost. I separate the cloves, keeping the skins intact, place them in the dirt with their pointy ends up, cover them with soil and then a heavy blanket of leaves, as if putting a child to bed, but saying good night for the winter.

Warm Spinach Dip

MANY OF THE RECIPES I CREATE ARE INSPIRED BY fresh, locally grown ingredients. This one, however, comes straight from my sister-in-law's kitchen where I tasted her traditional spinach dip made with sour cream and mayonnaise, and knew I would continue to crave it until I could create my own healthy alternative.

---

2 tablespoons extra virgin olive oil

½ cup chopped shallots

4 cups packed fresh spinach leaves

½ teaspoon sea salt

½ cup grapeseed oil mayonnaise

1 cup cooked cannellini beans

Ground white pepper

Gluten-free crackers of choice for serving

In medium skillet over medium-low heat, sauté shallots in olive oil until translucent (about 5 minutes). Add spinach and fold until leaves are just wilted. Remove from heat and transfer to food processor (leaving juices behind in skillet so dip does not become overly runny). Add salt, mayonnaise and cannellini beans and pulse until ingredients are just blended. Season to taste with white pepper and serve warm with crackers.

MAKES 2 cups

Marinated Mushrooms

MY MOTHER-IN-LAW TAUGHT ME how to make these savory mushrooms and they have been a staple appetizer ever since. I serve them with Artichoke Tapenade *(page 38)* and Smokey Eggplant Dip *(page 161)* for an antipasto that dissapears quickly.

¾ cup red wine vinegar

¾ cup extra virgin olive oil

1 tablespoon sea salt

1 tablespoon coconut sugar

1½ teaspoons freshly ground pepper

Pinch of red pepper flakes

¼ teaspoon dried oregano

½ teaspoon dried thyme or lemon thyme leaves

1 tablespoon minced red onion

2 garlic cloves, minced

Zest of 1 lemon

2 pounds cremini mushrooms

In large glass bowl with lid, combine all ingredients except mushrooms. Trim mushrooms, discard stem ends and cut halves into quarters. Add to bowl with marinade, cover and shake. Refrigerate and shake daily for 3 days before serving.

MAKES about 2 cups

Smokey Eggplant Dip

I WAS NEVER MUCH OF A FAN OF EGGPLANT until I discovered all the different varieties grown at my local organic farm. They come in all shapes and sizes, and any and all are delicious in this grilled baba ganoush-style dip.

---

1 small head garlic

Extra virgin olive oil

1 pound eggplant,
   any variety

3 tablespoons roasted tahini

Zest and juice of ½ small lemon

2 dashes of cayenne

2 dashes of paprika

⅛ teaspoon sea salt

1 teaspoon chopped fresh
   flat-leaf parsley

Preheat grill to medium high.

Rub garlic with olive oil, wrap in foil and place on outside edge of grill rack. Pierce each eggplant several times and place directly on grill. Grill until soft throughout, turning regularly to char on each side. Time will vary according to size and variety of eggplants used. When garlic and eggplant are soft, remove from heat and set aside until cool enough to touch.

Peel skin from eggplants and place flesh in food processor. Peel roasted garlic and place 3–4 cloves in food processor with eggplant. Add tahini, lemon zest, lemon juice and cayenne and pulse until just smooth. Season to taste with paprika, sea salt and extra garlic as desired (reserving remaining garlic for another use). Add parsley and pulse briefly to work into mixture. Remove from processor and serve garnished with a drizzle of extra virgin olive oil.

MAKES 1 cup

Pear Chutney

AT THE INSTITUTE OF SUSTAINABLE NUTRITION, students use all of their senses to create delicious, super-healing meals, without the help of actual recipes. They work with an abundance of locally sourced and foraged ingredients to yield incredible results, like this recipe.

---

2   pears, peeled, cored and diced

¼   cup chopped yellow onion

2   tablespoons grated fresh ginger

1   garlic clove, minced

1   tablespoon ground cumin

3   tablespoons maple syrup

2   tablespoons apple cider vinegar

Zest and juice of 1 lemon

Zest and juice of 1 orange

2   dashes of ground cinnamon

Dash of cayenne

Pinch of sea salt

In a medium pot over no heat, combine all ingredients. Turn heat to medium and cook until pears are soft (time will vary depending on ripeness of pears and size of dice). Remove from heat, mash mixture with the back of a fork until chutney is semi-smooth with some chunks of pear remaining. Serve or store refrigerated in airtight container.

MAKES about 1¼ cups

Pomegranate Ginger Cranberry Sauce

EVERY THANKSGIVING I MAKE ENOUGH cranberry chutney for the holiday, plus extra that I freeze to get us through winter. The one time I forgot to defrost the chutney in time to serve with our pot pie, I came up with this tangy alternative that took no time to prepare and was every bit as satisfying.

3   cups fresh cranberries

½   cup 100% pomegranate juice

¼   cup maple syrup

2   teaspoons grated fresh ginger

In pot over medium heat, bring cranberries and pomegranate juice to boil. Reduce heat to simmer, cover and cook for 5 minutes to soften berries. Stir in maple syrup and ginger and simmer 5 minutes longer. Remove from heat and set aside for 10 minutes to cool slightly and set before serving.

MAKES 3 cups

Love Your Belly Kraut

ONE TASTE OF HOMEMADE SAUERKRAUT was all it took to transform my former dislike of kraut to a newfound addiction. I don't know if it's the process, the taste or the probiotic strength that I like the most, but altogether they keep me fermenting regularly and including kraut in my diet (usually eating it straight from the jar).

TRADITIONAL KRAUT

2   medium green cabbages

3   tablespoons sea salt, plus more for brine as needed

2   tablespoons caraway seeds (optional)

SPICY RED KRAUT

1   small green cabbage

1   small red cabbage

½   cup grated or julienned daikon

½   cup thinly sliced red onion

2   tablespoons grated fresh ginger

2   tablespoons sea salt, plus more for brine as needed

TOOLS

3   wide-mouth quart-size canning jars with lids

1   large nonreactive bowl

Weights (anything that will fit inside your jar to keep cabbage submerged)

Cheesecloth and rubber bands

Core cabbages and slice into thin ribbons. Place in glass or ceramic bowl and sprinkle evenly with 1 tablespoon sea salt. If making spicy red kraut, add daikon, onion and ginger. Add remaining sea salt and massage cabbage deeply for about 10 minutes or until it releases its juices and reduces in volume by about half. For traditional kraut, fold in caraway seeds if desired.

Fill 3 wide-mouth quart-size canning jars approximately three-quarters of the way with firmly-packed cabbage (overfilled jars will likely bubble over during fermentation). Scrape down pieces of cabbage stuck to glass above the top of the kraut. Pour in cabbage juice remaining in bowl and place a weight in each jar to keep cabbage from floating to top of juice (spice jars make great weights). Cover with cheesecloth to keep out dust, wrap with rubber band to keep closed and set aside in cool, dry place out of direct sunlight.

Check and taste cabbage daily. If brine level has not risen above cabbage within 12–18 hours, make more brine by dissolving 1 teaspoon sea salt for each 1 cup water and pour enough brine into jars to submerge cabbage. Should brine dip below level of cabbage at any point, repeat this step. Any mold that appears can be skimmed off and discarded.

Fermentation can take as few as 5 days and up to multiple weeks. Shorter fermentation yields a crisp and fresh product while longer fermentation yields a softer, more sour result. I am partial to a 2-week ferment. When taste and texture are to your liking, put lids on jars, refrigerate and serve as desired.

MAKES 2½ quarts

Kimchi

KIMCHI WORKS ON THE SAME lacto-fermentation basis as sauerkraut, but is a much faster process as a result of pre-soaking the vegetables in brine before fermenting. While traditionally made with fish sauce, my vegan version delivers plenty of satisfying spice and tang.

1   head napa cabbage (about 1 pound)

1   head bok choy (about 1 pound)

2   carrots, thinly sliced

1   cup thinly sliced daikon

6   tablespoons sea salt, plus more as needed

6   cups water

6   scallions, coarsely chopped

1   yellow onion, chopped

5   garlic cloves, minced

3   tablespoons grated fresh ginger

3   chile peppers, seeded and minced

2   thumb-size pieces kombu

TOOLS

2   wide-mouth quart-size canning jars with lids

1   large nonreactive bowl

Weights (anything that will fit inside your jar to keep vegetables submerged)

Cheesecloth and rubber bands

Core and coarsely chop napa cabbage and bok choy and place in large glass or ceramic bowl with carrots and daikon. Dissolve salt in water and pour over vegetables so they are covered. If not covered, make more brine using 1 tablespoon salt for each cup water. Place a plate on vegetables to keep them submerged and set aside to soak for 3 hours.

In separate nonreactive bowl, mash together onion, garlic, ginger and chiles to form a paste. Drain brine from vegetables into separate bowl and reserve brine. Taste vegetables to see if they are good and salty. Add more salt if not salty enough, or rinse if you find them more than pleasantly salty. Add scallions and fold spice paste into vegetable mixture. Stuff into 2 wide-mouth quart-size canning jars. Wedge a piece of kombu into each jar. Pack vegetables firmly so brine rises above vegetables. If it does not, add some of the reserved brine.

Place juice glass or other nonreactive weight over vegetables to keep them submerged. Cover jars with cheesecloth, hold in place with rubber bands and set aside. Taste fermentation daily (I like a 4- to 6-day ferment). When kimchi tastes to your liking, remove weights, seal jars and refrigerate. Serve as desired.

MAKES 1½ quarts

Baked Kale Chips

EVEN IF YOU DON'T THINK YOU LIKE KALE, you're going to love kale chips, and they couldn't be easier to make. In fact, you may want to double this recipe, as they're likely to go fast once they're ready to eat.

1   large bunch kale

1   tablespoon extra virgin
    olive oil

¼   teaspoon sea salt

Freshly ground pepper

Preheat oven to 300°F. Line 2 baking sheets with parchment paper.

To remove stems of kale, hold stem with one hand and with other hand pinch base of leaves and slowly pull along stem toward top of leaf. Discard stems. Wash and dry leaves thoroughly and place in large bowl. Drizzle with olive oil, sprinkle with salt and massage into leaves. Add pepper to taste and spread kale out in single layer on prepared baking sheets. Place in oven and bake for 10–15 minutes or until kale is dry and crispy and just barely browned on the edges.

Remove from heat, transfer to bowl and serve.

SERVES 2

Dehydrated Kale Chips

DEHYDRATING TAKES KALE CHIPS to a whole new level of greatness. You can't go wrong with the chips on the previous page, but one taste of dehydrated kale and you'll never go back.

CHEESY

2	bunches kale
½	red bell pepper, chopped
¼	cup tahini or cashew butter
2	tablespoons chickpea miso
2	tablespoons nutritional yeast
2	tablespoons lemon juice
2	pinches of freshly grated nutmeg

CHILE

2	bunches kale
½	red bell pepper, chopped
1	garlic clove, peeled
¼	cup cashews
2	tablespoons lemon juice
2	tablespoons nutritional yeast
½	teaspoon chile powder
¼	teaspoon paprika
¼	teaspoon sea salt
	Dash of cayenne

FALAFEL

2	bunches kale
½	cup cooked chickpeas
3	tablespoons lemon juice
2	cloves garlic, peeled
2	tablespoons tahini
1	tablespoon extra virgin olive oil
1	teaspoon ground cumin
½	teaspoon ground coriander
½	teaspoon sea salt
	Dash of cayenne
	Pinch of ground cardamom

To make these dehydrated chips, you'll need a dehydrator or an oven that can be set as low as 125°F.

Remove and discard stem ends from kale but keep leaves whole. Wash and dry leaves thoroughly.

Select dressing, place all ingredients for that variety in food processor and process until smooth and creamy.

Place kale in large bowl, spoon on dressing and use your hands to rub dressing into leaves and coat evenly. Arrange leaves in single layers on dehydrator trays and dehydrate on 115–125°F for 4–6 hours or until crisp (time will vary based on temperature of dehydrator and size of leaves). Remove from dehydrator and serve or store in airtight container. (Alternatively, bake chips in preheated 125°F oven for 4–6 hours or until crisp.)

MAKES never enough!

Mushroom Soup with Caramelized Onions

COMBINE A RICH AND EARTHY MUSHROOM SOUP made without butter or cream with a savory and sweet onion soup made without melted cheese...and you have this surprisingly decadent soup.

½ cup thinly sliced fresh porcini mushrooms or ¼ cup dried

2 cups thinly sliced shiitake mushroom caps

1 cup thinly sliced chanterelle mushrooms

3 tablespoons extra virgin olive oil

3 large yellow onions, sliced into thin rings

3 garlic cloves, minced

3 tablespoons mirin

¼ teaspoon sea salt

½ teaspoon dried thyme

4 cups vegetable stock

Freshly ground pepper

3 tablespoons sweet white miso dissolved in ¼ cup water

PREPARING MUSHROOMS

Dried porcini mushrooms should be reconstituted by soaking in 1 cup hot water for 20 minutes. Remove mushrooms from water, but save soaking water. Chop mushrooms and set aside.

Wipe all fresh mushrooms with a just-damp sponge or towel to remove dirt. Remove and discard stems from shiitakes, slice caps into thin strips. Chop chanterelle stems and caps into ¼-inch pieces.

PREPARING SOUP

In a large cast iron skillet over medium heat, sauté onion in olive oil until evenly browned (about 10 minutes). Add garlic and mirin and sauté 2 minutes longer. Add fresh mushrooms and sauté until evenly browned (about 7 minutes). To avoid sticking, deglaze skillet with water 1 tablespoon at a time as needed. Stir in salt and thyme, remove from heat and transfer sautéed mixture to a medium Dutch oven.

If dried porcini were used, strain liquid from soaking mushrooms through cheesecloth to remove any dirt and add liquid to Dutch oven. Add vegetable stock and plenty of pepper. Simmer 5 minutes and remove from heat. Purée briefly with handheld blender to thicken base but leave majority of mushrooms whole. Allow soup to cool slightly before stirring in dissolved miso. Serve warm.

SERVES 6

Golden Parsnip Soup

I'M NOT SURE IF IT'S THE WARMING PEPPER FLAKES, the sweet parsnips or the sunny golden color of the turmeric, but put them all together in this soup, and they can warm me up and lift my mood on just about any cold winter day.

2   tablespoons virgin coconut oil

1   yellow onion, chopped

2   garlic cloves, minced

1   tablespoon grated fresh turmeric root (or 1 teaspoon ground)

2   teaspoons grated fresh ginger

2   tablespoons mirin

4   cups sliced parsnips

½   teaspoon sea salt, plus more to taste

4   cups vegetable stock or water

Red pepper flakes

Melt coconut oil in Dutch oven over medium-low heat. Add onion and garlic and sauté 3 minutes. Add turmeric, ginger and mirin and sauté 1 minute longer. Add parsnips, salt and vegetable stock and bring to boil. Reduce heat, cover and simmer until parsnips are soft (about 25 minutes depending on how thickly they are sliced).

Remove from heat and use handheld blender to purée soup until smooth. Season to taste with salt and serve topped with a pinch of red pepper flakes.

SERVES 4

Roasted Pumpkin Fennel Soup with Maple Pecans

MY GIRLS THINK OF THIS RECIPE as pumpkin pie for dinner. Roasting brings out a caramelized sweetness that makes this soup taste like you've fussed for hours…which you've not.

---

1 fennel bulb

1 yellow onion, halved and cut into wedges

3 garlic cloves, peeled

2 tablespoons plus 1 teaspoon extra virgin olive oil

1 3½-pound sugar pumpkin (about 4 cups cooked pumpkin)

¼ cup plus 2 tablespoons maple syrup

2 teaspoons maple sugar

Pinch of ground nutmeg

½ cup chopped pecans

Zest of ½ orange

4 cups vegetable stock

1 tablespoon apple cider vinegar

¼ teaspoon sea salt

Preheat oven to 425°F. Line 2 baking sheets with parchment paper.

Remove stalks and fronds from fennel bulb and discard. Cut bulb into thin wedges and place in bowl with onion wedges. Drizzle with 1 tablespoon olive oil and toss to coat. Spread onto one of the prepared baking sheets and set aside.

Prepare pumpkin by cutting in half, scooping out and discarding seeds. Rub outside of pumpkin with 1 teaspoon olive oil and place halves cut-side down on second baking sheet. Place both pumpkin and fennel mixtures in oven and roast 30 minutes or until soft. Toss fennel every 10 minutes to ensure even roasting. Remove from oven and set aside until cool enough to touch. Reduce oven temperature to 350°F.

In small bowl, combine 2 tablespoons maple syrup, maple sugar and nutmeg. Add pecans and fold to coat. Arrange pecans on a third parchment-lined baking sheet and bake 10 minutes. Remove from oven and set aside to cool and set.

Transfer roasted fennel and onion to large Dutch oven. Scoop out flesh from pumpkin (or peel away skin) and transfer to pot along with orange zest. Add vegetable stock and purée with handheld blender until smooth. Stir in apple cider vinegar, remaining ¼ cup maple syrup and salt and simmer to heat through. Remove from heat and serve topped with maple pecans.

SERVES 6

Sweet Potato Leek Soup with Sesame Sprinkle

I LOVE THIS SOUP ON ITS OWN, but add the sesame sprinkle and I simply can't get enough. It takes great control not to use the entire quantity just on my own serving.

1	leek
1	tablespoon extra virgin olive oil
1	teaspoon grated fresh turmeric root (or ½ teaspoon ground)
1	teaspoon grated fresh ginger
4	cups peeled and diced sweet potatoes
1	cup peeled and diced celery root (celeriac)

Vegetable stock

½	teaspoon sea salt
¼	teaspoon ground nutmeg
⅛	teaspoon ground white pepper
1	bay leaf

SPRINKLE

2 tablespoons sesame seeds

½ teaspoon sea salt

Generous pinch of ground nutmeg

Generous pinch of ground cinnamon

Generous pinch of paprika

Trim leek by cutting off and discarding root end and tops. Halve leek lengthwise, fan open stalk and rinse well. Chop white and light green portions only into ½-inch pieces.

In Dutch oven over medium-low heat, sauté leek in olive oil until soft, being careful not to brown. Add turmeric and ginger and stir. Add sweet potatoes, celery root and enough vegetable stock to just cover vegetables. Add salt, nutmeg and white pepper and submerge bay leaf. Bring to boil, reduce heat and simmer covered until vegetables are soft (about 20 minutes). Remove from heat and set aside to cool slightly and allow flavors to blend.

In small skillet over medium heat, toast sesame seeds until fragrant and lightly browned. Remove from heat and transfer to mortar. Add sea salt and grind with pestle until seeds start to break apart. Add nutmeg, cinnamon and paprika and grind to incorporate until mixture is half crumbs and half whole seeds.

Remove bay leaf and discard. Using handheld blender, purée soup until smooth and serve topped with spiced sesame seed sprinkle.

SERVES 4

Pumpkin and Cannellini Bean Chili

THERE I WAS, IN A SEA OF SHORT RIBS and barbecued beef at The Taste of Atlanta, when I stumbled upon Chef Dave sitting over an enormous pot of pumpkin chili. I was so excited that I dove blindly into his delicious chili...only to discover that it was full of sausage! To this day, I can't eat this chili without thinking of Chef Dave.

---

1   3½-pound sugar pumpkin (about 4 cups cooked pumpkin)

1   tablespoon extra virgin olive oil, plus more for rubbing pumpkin

1   onion, chopped

4   cloves garlic, minced

3   cups chopped tomatoes

3   cups cooked cannellini beans

2   cups water, plus more to thin as needed

2   teaspoons ground chile powder

1   teaspoon ground cumin

1   teaspoon sea salt

Freshly ground pepper

Ground cayenne or hot sauce

Preheat oven to 450°F. Line a baking sheet with parchment paper.

Cut pumpkin in half. Scoop out and discard seeds. Rub outside of pumpkin with olive oil and place halves cut-side down on baking sheet. Roast 40 minutes or until soft throughout. Remove from heat and set aside to cool.

In large Dutch oven over medium heat, sauté onion and garlic in olive oil for 3 minutes or until soft. Add tomatoes and cannellini beans and stir to combine. Scoop pumpkin out of its skin and add to pot. Add 2 cups water and stir to combine. Add chile powder, cumin, salt and pepper to taste. Stir and simmer for 10 minutes. Season to taste with cayenne or hot sauce. Thin to desired consistency with water and simmer 20 minutes longer. Remove from heat and serve.

SERVES 6

Celery Root Soup with Pepitas and Pomegranate

I SPENT YEARS IGNORING the gnarly-looking root otherwise known as celeriac, but when I finally brought it home, I was pleasantly surprised. Not only are its celery and parsley flavors delicious when roasted, but it makes this soup smooth, creamy and a breeze to prepare.

---

1   leek

1   tablespoon extra virgin olive oil, plus more for drizzling

2   garlic cloves, minced

2   large celery roots (celeriac), about 3 cups cubed

2   cups vegetable stock

1   cup rice milk

½   teaspoon sea salt

⅛   teaspoon ground white pepper

2   tablespoons salted roasted pepitas (hulled pumpkin seeds)

Seeds from ½ pomegranate

Trim off root end and dark green tops of leek. Halve leek lengthwise, fan open stalk and rinse well. Chop white and light green portions.

In Dutch oven over medium-low heat, sauté leek and garlic in 1 tablespoon olive oil until soft (about 4 minutes).

Cut off outer skin of celery root with knife (a peeler will never do). Chop root into cubes and add to pot with leek and garlic. Add vegetable stock, rice milk, salt and white pepper and stir to combine. Bring to boil, reduce heat and simmer covered for 20 minutes or until all vegetables are soft. Remove from heat and purée with hand-held blender until smooth. Serve topped with a drizzle of olive oil, a sprinkle of pepitas and pomegranate seeds.

SERVES 6

Spinach Salad with Orange Chile Dressing

MOST DAYS I FAVOR HEARTIER GREENS like kale and collards over spinach; but as a rich source of vitamin C, antioxidants and potassium, spinach is definitely worth including in the mix, especially when it tastes this good.

6	cups loosely packed spinach
2	oranges
2	avocados, peeled, pitted and sliced
½	small fennel bulb, cored and thinly sliced

DRESSING

2	tablespoons extra virgin olive oil
Zest and juice of ½ orange	
Zest and juice of 1 lime	
1	tablespoon maple syrup
½	teaspoon ground chile powder
¼	teaspoon ground cumin
Sea salt and freshly ground pepper	

Wash and dry spinach and place in serving dish. Cut skin and pith from orange and slice crosswise into thin rounds. Place on top of spinach along with avocado and fennel slices.

In small bowl, whisk together all dressing ingredients. Adjust seasoning to taste as desired. Drizzle over spinach salad and serve.

SERVES 6

Bitter Greens Salad with Warm Maple Pear Vinaigrette

A KILLER DRESSING CAN TURN ANY SALAD into a treat and this one qualifies hands down. I often have my children make our dressings as they're uninhibited by what they're "supposed" to use. But with this vinaigrette as my proof, some of their creativity has clearly rubbed off on me.

VINAIGRETTE

- 1 tablespoon extra virgin olive oil
- 2 garlic cloves, minced
- 1 small shallot, minced
- 1 pear (any variety), peeled and grated (about ¾ cup)
- 2 tablespoons maple syrup
- 1 tablespoon prepared mustard of choice
- 1 tablespoon lemon juice
- ¼ cup extra virgin olive oil

Sea salt

SALAD

- 6 cups watercress and/or arugula
- ½ Asian pear, cored and sliced into thin wedges
- 1 avocado, peeled, pitted and sliced into wedges
- ¼ cup roasted sunflower seeds

Heat olive oil in small skillet over medium heat. Add garlic and shallot and sauté 3 minutes. Add grated pear and continue sautéing until pear is soft and cooked through (about 3 minutes longer). Remove from heat and stir in maple syrup, mustard and lemon juice. Transfer to bowl, add olive oil and sea salt to taste and purée gently with handheld blender until just smooth. Set aside until ready to serve.

Place greens and sliced Asian pear in bowl and drizzle with desired amount of dressing. Toss to coat and place on individual serving plates. Top with avocado and sunflower seeds, and serve.

SERVES 6

Broccoli Salad with Dried Cranberries and Shallot Dressing

THE LURE OF DRIED CRANBERRIES never ceases to amaze me. Serve a straight broccoli salad and many kids turn up their noses. Add dried cranberries, and score!

1 bunch broccoli
   (2 medium heads)

4 cups boiling water

½ orange bell pepper,
   chopped

¼ cup juice-sweetened
   dried cranberries

2 tablespoons finely
   chopped red onion

½ cup slivered almonds,
   toasted

DRESSING

¼ cup extra virgin olive oil

1 small shallot, peeled and
   quartered

2 tablespoons apple cider
   vinegar

1 tablespoon plus
   1 teaspoon maple syrup

⅛ teaspoon sea salt

Freshly ground pepper

Prepare broccoli by cutting florets into small bite-size pieces. Peel stems and cut into similar size small pieces. Place in heatproof bowl and blanch by pouring boiling water over vegetables. Soak until florets are just bright green (about 20 seconds). Drain blanching water thoroughly and pat broccoli dry. Add bell pepper, cranberries and red onion and fold to combine.

In small bowl, combine olive oil, shallot, apple cider vinegar, maple syrup, salt and pepper to taste. Process with handheld blender until consistent and smooth. Adjust taste with extra salt and pepper as desired and pour over salad. Add toasted almonds and fold to evenly coat all ingredients. Serve warm.

SERVES 4

Brussels Sprout Slaw with Cranberries

I ADORE BRUSSELS SPROUTS roasted and sautéed, but never imagined I would like them raw…until now. This salad keeps well, so feel free to make extra for lunch tomorrow. You'll be glad you did.

---

4 cups trimmed and shaved Brussels sprouts (1 to 1½ pounds)

¼ small red onion

½ fennel bulb

2 tablespoons coarsely chopped juice-sweetened dried cranberries

2 tablespoons extra virgin olive oil

1 tablespoon apple cider vinegar

1 tablespoon lemon juice

Sea salt and freshly ground pepper

Use a mandoline or the thin-slicing blade on a food processor to slice sprouts into thin shavings and place in large bowl. Trim and discard root end and outer skin from onion, slice into similar-size thin shavings and add to bowl with sprouts. Trim and discard fennel stalks and core bulb. Slice similarly and add to bowl. Add cranberries and toss to combine all ingredients.

Drizzle olive oil, apple cider vinegar and lemon juice directly onto vegetables and fold to evenly distribute all ingredients. Set aside to sit for 20 minutes and allow vegetables to soften. Season to taste with salt and pepper, toss again and serve.

SERVES 4

VARIATION
This recipe presents the perfect opportunity to work Immune-Boosting Tonic Juice (page 152) into your diet. Simply substitute 2 tablespoons of tonic for the cider vinegar and lemon juice. Whisk together with olive oil, season to taste with salt and pepper, toss and serve.

Sautéed Greens Many Ways

I DON'T LIKE TO REPEAT RECIPES in my books, but have made an exception for dark leafy greens, since I prepare some combination of the following recipe almost daily. You can't go wrong adding a variety of greens to your menu, and your health will thank you.

---

2   bunches greens (kale, collards, chard, mizuna, bok choy, dandelion, mustard greens…)

1   tablespoon virgin coconut oil or extra virgin olive oil

1   tablespoon minced fresh garlic, ginger or turmeric (or any combination)

1   small onion, cut into wedges, or 1 leek (white and light green parts), halved and chopped

Sea salt or ume plum vinegar

Gomasio or toasted pumpkin seeds (optional)

Trim and discard dry stem ends from greens. If stems are particularly thick, pinch at bottom of leaves and pull up to separate stems from leaves. Save stems for making vegetable stock or discard. Chop greens into similar-size pieces.

In large Dutch oven or cast iron skillet over medium-low heat, sauté ginger and/or turmeric and/or garlic in oil until soft (about 2 minutes). Add onion or leek and sauté 2 minutes longer. Add chopped greens and fold until just wilted and bright green. Remove from heat and season to taste with sea salt or ume plum vinegar. Serve topped with a sprinkle of gomasio or toasted pumpkin seeds.

SERVES 4

Steamed Hakurei Turnips with Lemon and Sea Salt

I HAD NEVER MET A TURNIP I LIKED…until I met a Hakurei. Their sweet and mild flavor is delicious whether cooked or raw. This is my favorite way to enjoy them (other than straight off the farmstand) — gently steamed and delicately dressed, with or without their tender greens.

About 12 hakurei turnips

1 tablespoon extra virgin olive oil

Zest and juice of 1 Meyer lemon

Coarse sea salt and freshly ground pepper

Fit pot with steaming rack (or insert), add 1 inch of water and bring to boil. Trim and discard roots from turnips and cut off greens. Slice turnips in half and then into equal-size wedges. Place in pot and steam until just barely soft (about 4 minutes depending on size of wedges), adding greens for the final 2 minutes or until just bright green.

Transfer greens and turnips to bowl and toss with olive oil, lemon zest and lemon juice. Season to taste with sea salt and pepper and serve.

SERVES 6

Seared Tart Apple and Kale Sauté

IT'S FUNNY HOW INSPIRATION COMES. I needed a recipe to demo at a farmers market; vendors offered me their organic locally grown kale and apples…and voilà! It's hard to go wrong when you combine seasonal fresh produce.

---

2 teaspoons virgin coconut oil

½ small red onion, cut into thin wedges

1 tart apple (Macoun, Granny Smith or variety of choice), thinly sliced

Juice of ½ lemon

2 teaspoons grated fresh ginger

½ jalapeño, seeded and sliced into rings (optional)

1 large bunch kale, chopped

¼ teaspoon coarse sea salt

Melt coconut oil in cast iron skillet over medium-high heat. Add onion and sear until browned and barely soft (1–2 minutes). In bowl, toss apple slices with lemon juice, ginger and jalapeños (if using). Pour into skillet with onion and sear 1 minute on each side to lightly brown (apples will still be crisp on inside). Spoon apples and onions back into their original bowl.

Place kale in skillet and sauté until just soft and bright green, adding water 1 tablespoon at a time as needed to deglaze pan and steam kale. Remove skillet from heat and fold in onions and apples. Sprinkle with coarse sea salt, fold to combine and serve.

SERVES 4

Roasted Roots with Apple Cider Reduction

WHEN PLANTS DIE BACK IN THE FALL, their nutritional value goes down into the roots, resulting in produce that is super-healing and strengthening to our immune systems. Use this recipe as a template for experimenting with the many roots and tubers available.

1	medium rutabaga, peeled
6	hakurei turnips
1	large purple-top turnip
3	parsnips
3	burdock roots
2	small yams or sweet potatoes
6	shallots, peeled and halved
8	cloves garlic, peeled and halved
4–5	sprigs fresh thyme
½	teaspoon coarse sea salt
2	tablespoons extra virgin olive oil
1½	cups cooked chickpeas

REDUCTION

3	cups apple cider
1¼	cup apple cider vinegar
¼	cup maple syrup
5	whole cloves

Preheat oven to 450°F.

Chop rutabaga and place in large bowl. Scrub or peel turnips, parsnips, burdock and yams and cut into similar-size pieces. Add to bowl with rutabaga. Add shallots, garlic, thyme, salt and olive oil. Toss to combine and evenly coat all ingredients with oil. Pour into two 9 x 12-inch glass baking dishes and spread in single layer. Roast 20 minutes. Remove from oven, fold in chickpeas and roast 25 minutes longer (roots will be soft and lightly caramelized; chickpeas will be slightly crispy).

While roots are roasting, place all reduction ingredients in pot over high heat and bring to boil. Stir continuously until liquid reduces by half (about 30 minutes). Remove from heat and discard cloves.

Remove roots from oven and slide a spatula under vegetables to release anything sticking. Drizzle with reduction, toss and serve.

SERVES 4

Cauliflower Steaks with Ginger, Turmeric and Orange

NO MATTER HOW HARD I TRY, I still fall into the rut of serving the same few well-loved meals over and over. If I hadn't forced myself to buy one different produce item each week, I would have never discovered that my younger daughter is crazy for cauliflower. In the end, she's thrilled to have found a new food, and I'm recommitted to my one-new-food-a-week rule.

---

1   large head cauliflower

4   tablespoons extra virgin olive oil

1   teaspoon grated fresh ginger

1   teaspoon grated fresh turmeric root (or ½ teaspoon ground)

3   garlic cloves, minced

Zest and juice of 1 orange

Sea salt and freshly ground pepper

1   tablespoon chopped fresh cilantro

Preheat oven to 400°F. Line a baking sheet with parchment paper.

Remove leaves from cauliflower, trim base of stem and cut head from top down into ¾-inch slices, being careful not to detach florets from core. Save any outer florets that fall off for another use. Cut slices in half through core.

Heat cast iron skillet over high heat and cover bottom with 1½ tablespoons olive oil. Working in batches, place half of cauliflower steaks in skillet and sear each side 3 minutes or until lightly browned. Transfer to prepared baking sheet and repeat with second batch of cauliflower and 1½ tablespoons olive oil.

In small bowl, whisk together ginger, turmeric, garlic, orange zest, orange juice, remaining 1 tablespoon olive oil, and salt and pepper to taste. Brush on both sides of cauliflower steaks and roast for 15 minutes or until soft throughout. Remove from heat and serve topped with cilantro.

SERVES 4

SERVING SUGGESTION
Layer the cauliflower steaks over a bed of black lentils or wild rice.

Roasted Heirloom Tomato Sauce

After anxiously waiting much of the summer for my tomatoes to ripen, I'm always surprised when I reach that point where I just can't look at another tomato salad. That's when I turn to roasting. Roasted tomatoes bring a whole new level of satisfaction that carries me deep into the fall and is a great way to preserve my summer harvest.

4	pounds heirloom tomatoes (any and all varieties welcome!)
4	large cloves garlic, peeled
3	tablespoons extra virgin olive oil
1	teaspoon coarse sea salt
½	yellow onion, finely chopped
2	teaspoons minced fresh oregano leaves (or 1 teaspoon dried)
2	teaspoons minced fresh thyme leaves (or 1 teaspoon dried)
2	teaspoons minced fresh flat-leaf parsley leaves (or 1 teaspoon dried)
¼	cup red wine
	Sea salt and freshly ground pepper

Preheat oven to 350°F.

Cut tomatoes into similar-size large chunks and spread evenly into two 9 x 12-inch glass baking dishes. Add garlic, drizzle with 2 tablespoons olive oil and sprinkle with coarse sea salt. Place in oven and roast for 60 minutes or until skins shrivel and juices ooze. Remove from heat and set aside to cool.

In Dutch oven over medium heat, sauté onion in remaining 1 table-spoon olive oil for 2 minutes. Add oregano, thyme and parsley, reduce heat to medium-low and continue sautéing until translucent and slightly browned (about 5 minutes).

Place a mesh sieve over a Dutch oven. Peel skins from tomatoes, discard skins and place tomatoes in sieve. Use the back of a wooden spoon to press pulp and juices through to Dutch oven. Add any remaining juices from baking dishes. This will yield a seedless sauce. If you prefer a few seeds, transfer a few spoonfuls of pulp left in basket to Dutch oven. Add red wine, increase heat to medium and simmer 20 minutes. Season to taste with salt and pepper. Serve hot as desired or cool to room temperature, transfer to airtight containers and store in refrigerator or freezer.

MAKES about 3 cups

Quinoa with Roasted Beets and Celery Root

MY HUSBAND ENJOYS ALL OF THE MEALS I put on the table, but rarely eats the leftovers. The first time I made this recipe, he broke that pattern, calling dibs on all that remained to take for lunch the next day. I call that one powerful quinoa recipe!

1   cup tricolor quinoa

2   cups water

Pinch of sea salt

6   golden beets

2   celery roots (celeriac)

2   tablespoons extra virgin olive oil

¼   teaspoon sea salt

1   cup chopped toasted pecans

2   tablespoons chopped fresh flat-leaf parsley

DRESSING

3   tablespoons extra virgin olive oil

2   tablespoons red wine vinegar

1   shallot, minced

Zest and juice of 1 orange

2   teaspoons maple syrup

¼   teaspoon sea salt

Freshly ground pepper

Preheat oven to 400°F. Line 2 baking sheets with parchment paper.

Place quinoa in pot or rice cooker with water and salt. Bring to boil, reduce heat and simmer covered until water is absorbed (about 15 minutes). Remove from heat and set aside.

Peel beets, cut into ¾-inch cubes and place in bowl. Cut away and discard outside skin of celery root, cut bulb into similar-size pieces and add to bowl. Drizzle with olive oil, sprinkle with sea salt and toss to coat. Spread in single layers on baking sheets. Place in oven and roast 40 minutes or until tender, tossing occasionally to encourage even roasting. Remove from oven and set aside.

In small bowl, whisk together olive oil, red wine vinegar, shallot, orange zest, orange juice, maple syrup and sea salt. Season to taste with pepper and set aside.

Fluff quinoa and add roasted vegetables, toasted pecans and parsley. Pour dressing over quinoa, fold to evenly combine all ingredients and serve warm.

SERVES 6

Collard Green Sukiyaki with Buckwheat Noodles

THE FIRST TIME I MADE THIS SUKIYAKI, it barely made it off the stove. Ever since, I've served it in the skillet and let everyone fill a bowl with their favorite combination of veggies and noodles. There's never even a noodle left behind.

2½ cups water

2 dried shiitake mushrooms, broken into pieces

2 strips kombu

¼ cup tamari

¼ cup mirin

1 tablespoon maple syrup

8 ounces 100% buckwheat noodles (soba)

2 tablespoons sesame seeds

¼ teaspoon sea salt

8 whole collard leaves

1 tablespoon extra virgin olive oil

½ cup red onion wedges

½ cup julienned carrot

½ cup julienned daikon

¼ pound maitake mushrooms (or variety of choice), broken up

¼ cup water

In small pot, combine water, shiitake mushrooms and kombu. Bring to boil and press down on mushrooms and kombu so they stay submerged. Reduce heat and simmer 20 minutes. Scoop out and discard solids and stir in tamari, mirin and maple syrup. Simmer 5 minutes longer, remove from heat and set aside.

Cook noodles according to directions on package. Drain and set aside.

In small skillet, toast sesame seeds until lightly browned and fragrant. Remove from heat, transfer to mortar and add sea salt. Grind with pestle until seeds are half broken and mixture is well blended. Set aside.

Cut stems out of collard greens and stack leaves so they're all facing the same direction. Roll from one side to the other to form a log and cut crosswise into ¼-inch ribbons.

Heat large cast iron skillet over medium-high heat and add olive oil. Visually divide skillet into five pie slices and place one vegetable in each area—collard greens, onion, carrot, daikon and maitake mushrooms. Sauté 2 minutes pushing ingredients gently with a wooden spoon so that they don't stick but stay roughly in their defined area. Add water and simmer vegetables until collards are wilted (about 1 minute longer). Push ingredients closer to edge of pan and transfer cooked noodles to center of skillet.

Reheat shiitake-kombu stock and pour over noodles and vegetables. Sprinkle with sesame blend and serve.

SERVES 4

Brown Rice Veggie Patties

I MAKE MY VEGGIE PATTIES DIFFERENTLY EVERY TIME. I just can't limit myself to only a few set spices, and neither should you. Try different spices, vegetables, legumes and herbs until you find your favorite combination (and then pray you wrote it down as you were making it!). Just keep the same proportions as here, and don't leave out the rice.

¾ cup uncooked brown rice (to yield 1½ cups cooked)

1½ cups water

1 thumb-size piece kombu

1 tablespoon extra virgin olive oil

½ cup chopped red onion

4 garlic cloves, minced

¼ cup grated carrots

1 tablespoon mirin

½ cup cooked white beans (great northern or navy)

1 tablespoon dried oregano

1½ teaspoons paprika

1 teaspoon ground cumin

¼ cup chopped fresh flat-leaf parsley

½ teaspoon sea salt

¼ teaspoon freshly ground pepper

Preheat oven to 400°F. Line a baking sheet with parchment paper.

Place brown rice in pot or rice cooker with water and kombu. Bring to boil, reduce heat and simmer covered until water is absorbed (about 25 minutes). Remove from heat and set aside, but do not refrigerate. Remove and discard kombu.

In cast iron skillet over medium heat, sauté onion and garlic in olive oil until soft (about 3 minutes). Add carrots and mirin and sauté until carrots soften (2 minutes longer). Add beans, oregano, paprika, cumin, parsley, salt and pepper. Fold to combine and sauté to heat through. Fold in ½ cup cooked brown rice, remove from heat and set aside.

Place remaining 1 cup cooked brown rice in food processor and process until mushy. Transfer to skillet with vegetable-bean mixture and fold to evenly combine all ingredients. Batter will be quite sticky. Using your hands, form into 3-inch patties ½–¾-inch thick. Place on parchment-lined baking sheet and bake for 20 minutes. Remove from oven, carefully flip patties (press together as needed to keep patty form) and bake another 20 minutes. Remove from oven and serve.

MAKES 6 patties

Roasted Squash, Caramelized Shiitake and Shallot Lasagna

I AVOIDED PASTA FOR YEARS because it made me feel heavy and sluggish, but there are so many gluten-free varieties available now that don't have that same effect that I am happy to indulge. Not to mention, any time I can make a meal in advance, I'm a happy mom.

1	large butternut squash (3 to 4 pounds), halved and seeded
12	gluten-free lasagna sheets
2	tablespoons extra virgin olive oil, plus extra for drizzling
5	garlic cloves, minced
3	cups sliced shallots
½	pound shiitake mushrooms, stemmed and thinly sliced
3	tablespoons mirin
3	tablespoons minced fresh thyme leaves
6	cups spinach or arugula
¼	teaspoon sea salt
	Freshly ground pepper
2½	cups prepared tomato sauce of choice

Preheat oven to 350°F.

Place squash in a baking dish cut-sides down. Cover bottom of dish with ¼-inch water, cover with foil and bake 35 minutes or until squash is soft. Remove from oven and set aside until cool enough to touch. Scoop squash out of skin, transfer to medium bowl and set aside.

Cook pasta according to directions on package. When tender, drain, drizzle with enough olive oil to prevent sticking and set aside.

In large Dutch oven over medium heat, sauté garlic and shallots in olive oil until soft (about 3 minutes). Add shiitakes and sauté until mushrooms start to caramelize (about 5 minutes). Add mirin 1 tablespoon at a time to deglaze pan. Add thyme and sauté 1 minute longer. Fold in spinach, sauté until just tender (about 1 more minute) and season to taste with salt and pepper. Remove from heat and set aside.

In 10 x 13-inch baking dish, spread a layer of tomato sauce on bottom of pan. Add a layer of lasagna noodles followed by a layer of squash. Top with half the shiitake-spinach mixture, a layer of tomato sauce and another layer of noodles. Spread on another layer of squash, remaining shiitake-spinach mixture, more sauce and a final layer of noodles. Top with remaining squash and sauce, cover with foil and bake 35 minutes. Remove foil and bake 10 minutes or until the ingredients are bubbling. Remove from heat and set aside to cool slightly before serving.

SERVES 8

Fried Brown Rice and Cashews with Hot Sesame Oil

I AM THE QUEEN OF "UPCYCLING" FOOD — turning last night's leftovers into tonight's totally new and delicious dinner. This recipe is the ideal dish for "upcycling," as refrigerated leftover brown rice is the key to making perfect fried rice every time.

½   cup carrot rounds (⅛-inch thick)

½   cup sliced snow peas (cut crosswise on an angle into ¼-inch strips)

½   cup chopped scallions

1   shallot, minced

1-inch piece ginger, peeled and cut into thin strips

2   tablespoons mirin

2   tablespoons tamari

1   tablespoon virgin coconut oil

2   cups refrigerated cooked short-grain brown rice

2   teaspoons toasted sesame oil

½   teaspoon hot pepper sesame oil

4–5 dashes of ume plum vinegar

½   cup chopped toasted cashews

2   tablespoons chopped fresh cilantro

Prepare all vegetables, shallot and ginger and place on plate so they're ready to go. Add mirin and tamari to line-up.

Place wok or large cast iron skillet over high heat until water drizzled on surface sizzles and evaporates. Add coconut oil and tilt wok or skillet to coat cooking surface. Add shallot and ginger and stir-fry for 15 seconds. Continue stirring and add carrots. Fry until bright orange (about 30 seconds). Add snow peas, scallions and mirin. Add rice to vegetables and mash it with the back of your spatula or wooden spoon to break up any chunks. Fold to combine ingredients and heat through.

Push ingredients to edges of pan and add tamari to center. Push rice back into center to combine. Stir to evenly incorporate all ingredients and remove from heat. Drizzle with both sesame oils and ume plum vinegar. Fold in cashews, top with cilantro and serve.

SERVES 6

Kale and Roasted Sunchoke Pesto over Butterbeans

I GO TO THE FARM AS MUCH FOR THE PEOPLE as for the produce. The sense of community can't be beat, and the recipe idea sharing is like no place else. If you don't leave inspired and salivating, you likely don't have a pulse. I owe this one to Mariana, my soul sister in all things sustainably delicious.

---

1   cup dried butter beans (large lima beans)

1   thumb-size piece of kombu

Pinch of sea salt

PESTO

1   pound sunchokes, scrubbed and cut into ½-inch chunks

6   garlic cloves, peeled

¼   cup plus 2 teaspoons extra virgin olive oil

Sea salt and freshly ground pepper

2   cups chopped kale leaves (no stems)

½   cup pine nuts

2   tablespoons lemon juice

Place beans in bowl, cover well with water and soak overnight. When ready to cook, drain soaking water and rinse beans well. In Dutch oven, bring 6 cups water to boil. Add soaked beans, kombu and sea salt. When water returns to boil, reduce heat, and simmer covered until beans are soft throughout (about 50 minutes). Remove from heat and set aside.

Preheat oven to 400°F. Line baking sheet with parchment paper.

Place sunchokes, garlic and 2 teaspoons olive oil in bowl. Sprinkle with salt and pepper and toss to coat. Spread in single layer on prepared baking sheet. Place in oven and roast 30 minutes or until soft. Remove from oven and transfer to food processor. Add kale, pine nuts, lemon juice and ½ teaspoon sea salt. Turn processor on and slowly pour in ¼ cup olive oil. Turn processor off, scrape down sides and process again until pesto is smooth.

Drain beans, discard kombu and return beans to Dutch oven. Spoon pesto over beans, fold to combine and serve warm.

SERVES 4 (makes 1¼ cups pesto)

French Lentils with Shiitakes and Brussels Sprouts

THE MOST PRIZED POSSESSION in my kitchen is my cast iron skillet, which yields delectable caramelized vegetables. You may be tempted to skip the lentils in this recipe…until you taste this great combination.

½ cup French lentils

1 cup water

Sea salt

3 tablespoons extra virgin olive oil

½ pound shiitake mushrooms, stemmed and thinly sliced

4 shallots, sliced

12 medium Brussels sprouts, trimmed and cut into ¼-inch slices

1 tablespoon mirin

1 teaspoon dried thyme

Zest of ½ lemon

Freshly ground pepper

Place lentils in pot or rice cooker with water and a pinch of sea salt and bring to boil. Reduce heat and simmer covered until liquid is absorbed and lentils are tender (about 35 minutes). Remove from heat and cool without fluffing (so lentils don't mush).

In large cast iron skillet over high heat, heat 2 tablespoons olive oil. Add shiitake mushrooms and sear until mushrooms are evenly browned (about 5 minutes). Stir only enough to prevent sticking (overstirring will make mushrooms soft but not browned). Remove mushrooms from skillet, place in bowl and set aside.

Reduce heat to medium and add remaining tablespoon olive oil to skillet. Add shallots and sauté until they start to brown (about 2 minutes). Add Brussels sprouts and sauté 2 minutes. Add mirin and continue sautéing until Brussels sprouts are bright green (about 3 minutes). Return mushrooms to skillet along with thyme and sauté to heat through. Fluff lentils and fold into mushroom-sprout mixture. Add lemon zest, ¼ teaspoon sea salt and plenty of pepper. Fold to combine, remove from heat and serve.

SERVES 4

Portobellos Topped with Cannellini Bean Mash and Brussels Sprout Ribbons

THIS IS MY TAKE ON A GOURMET BURGER. Roasted portobello mushrooms are hearty and deliciously juicy. With herbed cannellini beans instead of bread, and pan-seared Brussels sprouts instead of lettuce, you'll wonder how anyone could prefer a burger in the first place.

4	portobello mushrooms
4	teaspoons extra virgin olive oil, plus extra for rubbing
2	teaspoons fresh or dried thyme leaves
Sea salt and freshly ground pepper	
2	shallots, minced
3	garlic cloves, minced
2	teaspoons herbes de Provence
1½	cups cooked cannellini beans
6	Brussels sprouts
Paprika	

Preheat oven to 400°F. Line a baking sheet with parchment paper.

Wipe mushroom caps with a damp sponge, remove and discard stems and rub both sides with olive oil. Place mushrooms gill-side up on prepared baking sheet. Sprinkle with thyme, sea salt and pepper. Place in oven and roast 15 minutes or until soft and juicy (time will depend on size of caps). Turn off oven and leave mushrooms inside to stay warm.

In skillet over medium heat, sauté shallots and garlic in 2 teaspoons olive oil for 1 minute. Add herbes de Provence and continue sautéing until soft (about 2 minutes). Add cannellini beans and sauté until heated through. Remove from heat and use the back of a wooden spoon or potato masher to mash and combine ingredients. Season to taste with salt and pepper, cover and set aside.

Prepare Brussels sprouts by thinly slicing from the top down into ribbons. In small skillet over medium heat, sauté ribbons in remaining 2 teaspoons olive oil until just bright green (about 1 minute).

Remove mushrooms from oven and place on serving platter or individual plates gill-side up (be careful not to spill juices out of caps). Top each mushroom with one-quarter of mashed bean mixture, a sprinkle of paprika and one-quarter of the Brussels sprout ribbons, and serve.

SERVES 4

Simple Black Lentils with Onion and Cilantro

IT'S QUITE POSSIBLE THAT BLACK LENTILS are one of my favorite legumes. I eat them warmed for breakfast with a little chopped avocado, tossed with roasted roots or sautéed greens for lunch, or topped with cauliflower steaks and fresh parsley for dinner. They are quick and easy to prepare, easy to digest and super-satisfying.

---

1 cup black lentils

3 cups water

Pinch of sea salt

2 tablespoons extra virgin olive oil

1 yellow onion, chopped

1 tablespoon red wine vinegar

1 teaspoon ground cumin

2 tablespoons chopped fresh cilantro

Sea salt and freshly ground pepper

Place lentils in pot with water and salt. Bring to boil, reduce heat and simmer covered until soft (about 20 minutes). Remove from heat and set aside.

Meanwhile, in small skillet over medium heat, sauté onion in 1 tablespoon olive oil until very soft (about 5 minutes). Remove from heat, stir in remaining 1 tablespoon olive oil, red wine vinegar, cumin and cilantro. Season to taste with salt and pepper.

Pour sautéed onion mixture over lentils, fold to combine and serve.

SERVES 4

Pan-Seared Crispy Tempeh

IF I'M GOING TO EAT SOY, I stick with organic, fermented soybean products. Tempeh is my favorite, but certain members of my family aren't such big fans. Instead of fighting a losing battle, I keep all of the tempeh to myself, favoring simple preparations like this one that I can make as part of an easy, delicious and nutritious lunch.

¼ teaspoon ground turmeric

Generous pinch of mustard powder

Generous pinch of sea salt

Generous grind of pepper

8 ounces tempeh

3 tablespoons extra virgin olive oil

2 tablespoons lemon juice

In small bowl, combine turmeric, mustard, salt and pepper.

Heat 1 tablespoon olive oil in cast iron skillet over high heat. Add tempeh in single layer and sear 30 seconds. Drizzle 1 tablespoon olive oil and 1 tablespoon lemon juice evenly over tempeh and sprinkle on half of the spice mixture. Flip tempeh, drizzle remaining 1 tablespoon olive oil and remaining 1 tablespoon lemon juice over second side of tempeh and sprinkle on remaining spices. Sear until crispy and browned (about 1 minute), sliding pan back and forth on burner a few times to keep tempeh from sticking and encourage even searing. Flip one last time to make opposite side equally browned and crisp (if necessary). Remove from heat and serve.

SERVES 2

SERVING SUGGESTIONS
Serve with mixed green salads, sautéed greens or roasted vegetables.

Blondies

I DON'T RECALL WHEN I FIRST TASTED A BLONDIE BAR, but I've been able to conjure up the memory of that taste every day since. Brown sugar, butterscotch, chocolate chunks…I think I've spent most of my life craving these rich and gooey delights. All I can say about this recipe is that it's been worth the wait.

WET INGREDIENTS

1 cup cooked cannellini beans

½ cup sunflower butter

¼ cup plus 2 tablespoons applesauce

3 tablespoons virgin coconut oil, melted

2 teaspoons vanilla extract

⅓ cup maple syrup

DRY INGREDIENTS

1 cup almond flour/meal

½ cup millet flour

¾ cup coconut palm sugar

¼ teaspoon sea salt

2 teaspoons baking powder

½ cup gluten-free dark chocolate chunks

Preheat oven to 350°F. Lightly grease a 9 x 12-inch baking pan.

Place all wet ingredients in food processor and process until smooth.

In separate bowl, combine almond flour, millet flour, coconut sugar and sea salt. Fold in baking powder and add to food processor. Process to combine all ingredients and yield thick batter. Pour into baking pan and sprinkle with chocolate chunks. Using a spatula, press the chunks into batter and smooth top.

Place in oven and bake 30 minutes. Remove from heat and set aside to cool before removing from pan. These blondies will require a gentle touch when cutting. Wash knife if cake sticks to blade and continue with a clean edge. Cut into squares…and inhale.

MAKES about 20 blondies

Applesauce Cake

I'VE BEEN TRYING TO RECREATE my dear friend Vicki's apple cake for years. At last, Vicki has shared her recipe. I took out the butter and sugar, but kept the memories of sharing this with our families.

Virgin coconut oil

BASE

1½ cups almond flour/meal

½ cup coconut flour

¼ teaspoon sea salt

¼ teaspoon baking soda

¼ cup maple syrup

3 tablespoons extra virgin olive oil

1 tablespoon lemon juice

1 tablespoon water

½ teaspoon vanilla extract

FILLING

4 cups peeled and shredded apples

½ cup maple syrup

2 teaspoons lemon juice

½ teaspoon ground cinnamon

2 tablespoons almond flour/meal

2 tablespoons coconut flour

TOPPING

3 apples

1 tablespoon lemon juice

1 tablespoon maple syrup

1 teaspoon vanilla extract

⅛ teaspoon ground cinnamon

½ cup apricot fruit spread

Preheat oven to 350°F. Lightly grease a 9-inch springform pan with coconut oil and line bottom with a round of parchment paper.

PREPARING BASE

In large bowl, combine almond flour, coconut flour, salt and baking soda. In separate bowl, whisk together maple syrup, olive oil, lemon juice, water and vanilla. Pour wet ingredients into dry and fold to combine. Press into springform pan and bake 14 minutes or until edges start to brown. Remove from heat and set aside.

PREPARING FILLING AND TOPPING

In large bowl, combine shredded apples, maple syrup, lemon juice, cinnamon, almond flour and coconut flour. Spread evenly over crust.

Peel and cut apples into ⅛-inch thick slices and place in shallow bowl. In separate bowl, whisk together lemon juice, maple syrup, vanilla and cinnamon. Pour over apple slices and toss to coat. Arrange slices on top of filling in a fanlike pattern. Place pan on baking sheet and bake 1 hour. Remove from oven and cool before removing springform pan.

In small pot over medium heat, melt apricot preserves. Paint evenly on top of cake to finish and serve.

SERVES 8

Apple Goji Berry Fruit Leather

GOJI BERRIES ARE PACKED WITH ANTIOXIDANTS making this more than just a tasty treat, and you'll have yourself a good laugh when you take this leather out of your dehydrator and discover that it looks a bit like bacon. In early summer I use fresh mulberries from the tree at the farm instead of goji berries.

4 cups peeled, chopped baking apples

1 cup dried goji berries

1 teaspoon lemon juice

Maple syrup (optional)

Place apples and goji berries in pot with 1 inch water. Bring to boil, reduce heat, and simmer covered until both apples and berries are soft (time will vary according to size of chunks). Remove from heat and drain (reserve cooking liquid for another use).

Transfer cooked fruit to food processor and process until smooth. Add lemon juice and pulse to combine. Taste mixture and add maple syrup 1 tablespoon at a time until desired sweetness is achieved. Return mixture to pot and simmer over low heat until thick (3–5 minutes).

Set up dehydrator or preheat oven to as close to 125°F as possible.

Line dehydrator trays or 2 rimmed baking sheets (if using oven) with parchment paper. Pour fruit purée onto trays or baking sheets and spread evenly just slightly more than ⅛-inch thick. Place in dehydrator or oven and dehydrate approximately 7 hours or until dry throughout.

Remove from dehydrator or oven, lift paper off trays and place on cutting board. Score through leather with knife to cut and then peel strips off paper. Roll in parchment paper and store in airtight container.

MAKES 4 dehydrator trays or 2 standard baking sheets of fruit leather

Maple Cinnamon Cookies

MY GIRLS CALL THESE "CINNAMON BUN COOKIES." The aroma alone draws them to the kitchen whenever I bake them, and we have a hard time making them last longer than just out of the oven.

DRY INGREDIENTS

1 cup almond flour/meal

1 cup millet flour

1½ teaspoons ground cinnamon

1 teaspoon baking powder

¼ teaspoon sea salt

WET INGREDIENTS

½ cup cashew butter

½ cup maple syrup

¼ cup plus 2 tablespoons applesauce

2 tablespoons virgin coconut oil, melted

1 teaspoon vanilla extract

Maple sugar (or shaved Tonewood® Maple Cube)

In bowl, whisk together dry ingredients.

Place all wet ingredients in food processor and process to blend. Pour in dry ingredients and process to form consistent batter. Transfer to bowl, cover with parchment paper and press down on paper so that it sticks to and seals batter. Refrigerate 1–2 hours.

Preheat oven to 350°F. Line baking sheet with parchment paper.

Remove batter from refrigerator, scoop by the tablespoon and drop onto prepared baking sheet. Press down gently with back of spoon to flatten cookies just slightly. Sprinkle each with maple sugar and bake cookies 18 minutes. Remove from oven and cool on wire rack.

MAKES 15 cookies

Roasted Maple Balsamic Pears

THESE WARM AND CARAMELIZED PEARS are about to become your go-to fall dessert. We like them served over coconut non-dairy ice cream, and I always make extra to enjoy over steel cut oats in the morning.

4   ripe pears, Bosc or d'Anjou
1   teaspoon virgin coconut oil
2   tablespoons maple syrup
2   tablespoons balsamic vinegar
1   tablespoon lemon juice
Zest and juice of 1 orange
¼   cup sliced almonds, toasted

Preheat oven to 400°F.

Quarter pears by cutting from stem to base. Using a melon baller, scoop out and discard core. Melt coconut oil in cast iron skillet over medium heat. Place pears flesh-side down and sauté 3 minutes on each side until lightly browned.

In small bowl, whisk together maple syrup, balsamic vinegar, lemon juice, orange zest and orange juice. Add almonds and drizzle mixture evenly over pears.

Transfer skillet to oven and bake 10 minutes or until pears are soft and caramelized. Remove from oven and serve.

SERVES 6

WINTER

THE GIFT THAT GIVES AS MUCH AS IT TAKES

Gone are the healing sunlight, the fresh produce and the long relaxing days—the lifelines that sustain our mental and physical health. There is no choice but to go inside where it is warm and safe, and where we are faced with the greatest challenge of all—nourishing ourselves from within. For many, the holidays provide the perfect entry to the deep and meaningful work of the season. They enrich our lives with connection and reflection and remind us to give thanks—the very foundations of a mindfulness practice. Once passed, the cold and isolating days of winter stretch out before us with spring a journey away. The flavors and tastes that enlivened us just months ago are replaced with the sweet and satisfying foods of winter—the roots that ground us, the squashes that warm and comfort, the preserved foods that keep alive the faint memory of the seasons past, and the fermented foods that awaken us internally and support our prolonged health. Winter is the season of simplicity and survival, full of opportunities to reconnect with the healing stillness and the peace that is inside of us. All this time we thought winter was taking away life, but, rather, it was opening the door to discovering the healing light within.

CONTENTS

Maintaining Balance

At winter's start, I am grateful for the shorter days, the quiet, and the warm and comforting foods. Months later, I have had enough, and it seems like many seasons have passed in between. There is an inward focus to winter that can be renewing and restorative if we embrace it. While there are natural challenges, from the cold to spending so much time indoors, this is an ideal time to take inventory, slow down and look within.

STRATEGIES FOR SURVIVAL

In other seasons, the bounty of fresh vegetables increases every day. In winter, it decreases. We start with abundance from the harvest and the holidays and end with a scarcity of fresh produce. While the aim is to stay on a healthy course, the stress of the season can make us give in to instant gratification rather than make the healthy choice.

When I meditate, as soon as I am aware of having thoughts, I usher them out and return to my mantra. The trick is realizing that you've wandered in the first place. Eating clean and navigating this season without imbalance and regret requires the same discipline. Once you realize you've gone off course, reconnect with the following strategies to help you get back on track.

Review clean eating goals…and recommit to bringing in all the tastes and colors, with extra emphasis on dark leafy greens.

Set yourself up for success…there will be plenty of temptations around every turn, so make your home a safe zone. Plan meals ahead of time and keep your pantry and refrigerator well stocked for healthy breakfasts, vegetable-based meals, cleansing greens and blood sugar-stabilizing legumes.

Don't skip meals…whether home or out, fill your plate with fresh vegetables that help maintain energy, positive mood and physical balance.

Never show up hungry…so you have the strength to avoid impulse eating and splurges you'll regret later. Keep cravings for non-nutritional sweets at bay by incorporating plenty of nutritional sweets (carrots, squash, pears, pomegranate…).

Share the journey…sounds much nicer than "be accountable," but it's the same thing. Little can keep us from making bad choices like knowing that someone is watching. Sometimes it helps to ask for support, other times it serves us better to journal and be accountable only to ourselves.

Slow down…and practice meditation, yoga or whatever it is that helps you relieve stress so that when faced with choices you'll be better able to breathe in and reconnect with healthy intentions.

Practice self-care…a little more exercise, a long walk, a massage, extra sleep and time for the people and things you care about can help keep the scale of life balanced even when challenged to tip in the other direction.

Spend time outdoors…and be part of the season so you don't feel like you're fighting against it. Let the season invigorate you, not bring you down.

Let life nourish you…so food doesn't have to do all the heavy lifting.

Embrace all of your choices…and enjoy every bite. Nobody is served by self-judgment and negative thoughts. Going easy on yourself is a great and healing gift.

Winter Self Care

Taking care of ourselves in winter may require some extra attention, whether addressing mind, body or soul. Spending so much time indoors, we can't help but be exposed to more germs in winter. I've outlined a number of tools to maintain good health all year long, but I have a special toolbox just for winter.

Vitamins I fill my plate with nutrient-rich foods to support good health all winter long, loading up on vitamin C-rich dark leafy greens and lemons, sprinkling pumpkin seeds high in zinc on my salads, eating avocados and almonds for vitamin E, lacto-fermented foods for good bacteria to keep my gut healthy and strong, brewing teas for immune-supporting roots and herbs, and even eating mushrooms for vitamin D to compensate for reduced exposure to the sun. Clean food is always the best source of good nutrition, but sometimes supplements, based on a doctor's recommendation, can help provide balance when the body is symptomatic.

Hydration Cold temperatures, wind and forced air heat can leave us particularly dehydrated. Go easy on your organs and drink plenty of room-temperature water, water with lemon or tea.

Teas Teas have been used for thousands of years to treat illness. By combining different teas and herbs we can create an infinite number of healing blends that will not only soothe, but will support good health. A cup of tea can satisfy my cravings for something sweet, give me comfort, warm me from the inside out, take the place of a snack, curb my appetite, settle my stomach, improve my mood and help me sleep better. There are many prepared and packaged tea blends that you can start with, but blending your own can open up a world of tastes and opportunities for good health. Perhaps best of all, what I like about tea is that I actually have to stop what I'm doing in order to sit down and enjoy it. If that isn't living well, I don't know what is!

Tongue scrapers Every natural healer I've ever consulted with has asked to look at my tongue. Talk about making a person feel self-conscious! Eastern traditions believe that the body's state of health is reflected in the different regions and characteristics of the tongue. By scraping, we can help maintain oral health and remove the bacteria

Some of my favorite teas and herbs include:

Astragalus – for powerful immune support.

Chamomile – a natural sedative for settling the stomach and nerves, and treating menstrual cramps.

Cinnamon – for antibacterial and antifungal properties as well as for improving circulation, regulating blood sugar and cholesterol, and relieving nausea and gas.

Dandelion – for liver health and purifying blood.

Echinacea – for antibacterial properties to boost immune strength, reduce inflammation and help treat the common cold.

Ginger – for settling an upset stomach, aiding digestion, reducing inflammation and treating colds.

Green tea – rich source of antioxidants that help lower cholesterol, regulate blood sugar, improve memory and boost metabolism.

Lemon balm – for indigestion, anxiety and aiding sleep.

Lemongrass – for supporting digestion and circulation, helping with cramping, and calming nerves.

Lemon verbena – for calming nerves, boosting metabolism and aiding digestion.

Nettles – for strengthening the immune system, reducing inflammation and mucus, and treating allergies and a host of other ailments.

Peppermint – for improving digestion, relieving stress, breaking up mucus and helping diffuse headaches.

Rooibos – rich source of minerals and antioxidants for treating allergies and hay fever.

Rosehips – a rich source of vitamin C to support the immune system and adrenal function.

Rosemary – for improving circulation, regulating blood pressure, boosting energy and relieving gas, headache and muscle pain.

White tea – for immune support and potent anticancer properties.

that cause bad breath, decay and gum disease. It's my hope that if my tongue reflects what's going on inside of me, perhaps the reverse is true too, and I can influence my health by keeping my tongue clean. From personal experience, brushing the tongue moves everything around but does not necessarily remove it. Scraping is easy, effective, and slightly addictive once you get the hang of it.

Neti pot There's intentional repetition here in case you're like me and use your neti pot for spring allergies, and then forget you have it until you're multiple days into a sinus cold! *(See Spring, page 29)*.

Skin Care Skin can take a beating during winter. Stay extra hydrated on the inside to keep skin moist on the outside, and eat a nutrient-rich diet. Bringing in good fats (avocados, nuts, seeds…), drinking plenty of room-temperature or warm water, and getting ample sleep will help maintain healthy skin. Your skin is your largest organ and needs to be cared for. Slough skin regularly to remove dead skin and finish your shower with cold water to close pores, improve circulation and metabolism, and activate the immune system. Massage skin regularly with a safe, toxin-free moisturizer (you can find a list at EWG.org), organic virgin coconut oil or apricot oil.

Exercise Winter may throw a curve ball in the direction of your exercise routine, so use the opportunity to try something new, or maybe just return to an activity you haven't done in a long time. Switching it up helps keep us from getting bored and provides cross-training that supports balanced fitness, strong muscles and strong bones. Get your heart pumping each day to support cardiovascular health, maintain healthy weight, improve mood, increase energy, improve sleep and support good health in general.

Giving

ift giving can nourish both the giver and the receiver. Homemade and homegrown gifts not only show someone how much you care, but leave a smaller footprint in the process. Gifts that support good health are even more precious and sustainable on all levels. I remember what an honor I felt the first time a friend gave me her homegrown hardneck garlic. Now *that* says love!

Next time you want to give a gift, skip the manufacturer, the packaging, the gas to get to the store and the gift wrap that will end up in the landfill, and look to the pantry. A supply of jars makes homemade gift giving especially easy, is a great way to recycle jars and sometimes is a gift all on its own.

Some of my favorite health-giving gifts:

Dried herbs (and herb blends from my garden)
Baked goods (especially my Nutty Granola, *page 17* and NoNo Bars, *page 272*)
Immune-Boosting Tonic (*page 152*)
Sauerkraut (*page 165*)
Kimchi (*page 166*)
Fermented radishes (and other vegetables, *page 41*)
Dehydrated foods (especially tomatoes and hot peppers from my garden)
Teas and tea blends (see previous page)
Hot cocoa blends (with raw cacao, fresh spices and chile pepper)
Vanilla extract (see next page)

ENTERTAINING

Entertaining brings much welcome connection and cheer into our lives and homes that helps balance the solitude of winter. Create a menu in advance, plan time to prepare, enroll the help of others and cook as much love and good intention into your meal as possible. A shared meal has healing power beyond the food, so indulge. Here are some tips for creating a festive shared meal.

Pick a theme. Let go of what you feel you should serve, and discover what it is you want to serve, perhaps based on a tradition, a favorite recipe or ingredient, a particular region…. Sometimes just bringing friends together is theme enough.

Develop the menu. Certain recipes just beg to be prepared. If something speaks to you, that's the best place to start. In winter, my menus often feature foods preserved from fall such as roots and squashes, dried grains and legumes and fermented and frozen foods.

Consider presentation. Serving a rainbow of color will assure a beautiful plate as well as balanced nutrition and taste.

Make a list. Start with the ingredients (by recipe), then drinks and extras (candles or flowers), then items to prepare in advance and finally chores (like cleaning). A timeline can also be helpful to keep you organized and in control.

Focus on what's important. Keep it simple and achievable. Guests don't care if you're Wonder Woman or Superman, they just want to share the time and meal. Many guests don't like to show up empty-handed, so don't hesitate to ask for or accept help.

Breathe. Nothing sets the tone better than sharing what's in your heart, and all will enjoy themselves more when the host is relaxed and fully present.

HOMEMADE VANILLA EXTRACT

I had never made my own vanilla extract until it was taught at The Institute of Sustainable Nutrition. Now I'll never go back to store-bought. Vanilla beans can be used repeatedly, making this a pure, delicious and even economical gift for yourself or your friends. (See *A Few of My Favorite Things, page 275*, for resources to purchase vanilla beans and apothecary bottles.)

4   vanilla beans
2   4-ounce dark-colored apothecary bottles
1   cup organic vodka

With a sharp knife, score beans down middle, peel open and flatten. Use tip of spoon to scrape seeds out of each bean and divide between two bottles. Cut remaining beans into 3 pieces and add to bottles. Fill each bottle with vodka, cover and label, including date. Set aside to infuse, and shake daily.

My dear friend calls shaking the bottle "giving it the love." In the early days of winter I start my mornings coming down to my dark kitchen and "giving the love" to all of my bottles of vanilla and immune-boosting tonic. This has to result in a more healing product than simply shaking!

Vanilla will be ready for use after 2 months. When extract starts to run out, top the bottle up with vodka and let it infuse for 2 more months (for this reason, it's good to keep 2 bottles—one for active use and one for infusing). The same beans can infuse multiple refills. When vanilla loses its potency, it's time for new beans.

Experiment with different varieties of vanilla beans and different alcohols for different flavors. Imagine vanilla extract made with bourbon to bake figs and peaches, or made with rum to bake mango and pineapple. Yum!

Planting Seeds

Fresh produce always does the body and mind a whole lot of good, and winter doesn't have to be a time of going without. Hoop houses and greenhouses make winter farming possible in most zones. Farmers markets are fewer and further between, but do exist and can satisfy your craving not only for fresh produce, but for community and connection. The greatest challenge will be to find and support these farms and farmers. The same online resources you used in spring can help you locate farms that operate year-round, farmers markets, food hubs, coops and even services that distribute produce and products *(see page 275)*.

Growing your own is also still an option in winter. A countertop that gets the direct sun can support growing baby greens and herbs such as rosemary, thyme and oregano. Sprouts are another option for indoor growing and require only a little space and effort.

Sometimes it can feel like a large enough task just taking care of my own health during winter, let alone growing food. Even if there's nothing growing on my counters, winter is valuable time to plan and prepare for spring.

Plan a garden. Determine where you want to garden—perhaps in your yard, in pots on a porch or at a community garden. Measure out your space and decide what you want to grow. Check out a variety of seed catalogs, research local farmers or farm stores to find who sells organic seedlings and make a wish list. Last but not least, order your seeds.

Research Community Supported Agriculture (CSA). Search online, inquire at your local health food store or visit your local chamber of commerce to learn about CSAs available near you and start calling. Farms often sell their shares long before the growing season begins, so act early.

Volunteer. Even if we never grow one green leaf, time spent volunteering on a local farm connects us more meaningfully with the source of our food, and fosters understanding and appreciation for quality, locally grown produce.

Plant your seeds. Schedule seed planting based on the guidelines on the seed pack. Start early seeds indoors, pull them into the sun by day and back indoors by night. Or, direct sow early crops in your garden as soon as appropriate for your plant hardiness zone.

THOUGHTS OF SPRING

Contemplating our choices for eating clean and living well can be as important and empowering as acting on them. Winter is not a reason but rather an opportunity to take extra care of yourself and your family, and to be gentle, slow and mindful. Keep it simple, get a lot of sleep, honor your body and your process, and get ready. Spring and all of its promise will be here before you know it.

Gomasio

THIS TRADITIONAL JAPANESE CONDIMENT imparts big taste and significant health benefits. A rich source of minerals and cholesterol-lowering phytosterols, this is an easy way to add taste and healing power to your diet. I start with the traditional blend of sesame seeds and salt and mix it up from there with my favorite herbs and spices.

TOASTED NORI AND GARLIC

- 2 tablespoons unhulled sesame seeds
- ½ teaspoon sea salt
- ¼ teaspoon garlic powder
- 1 pinch of toasted nori flakes

CUMIN GINGER

- 2 tablespoons unhulled sesame seeds
- ½ teaspoon sea salt
- ¼ teaspoon ground cumin
- ¼ teaspoon ground ginger
- ⅛ teaspoon paprika

CACAO CHILE

- 2 tablespoons unhulled sesame seeds
- ½ teaspoon sea salt
- ½ teaspoon raw cacao powder (or 1 teaspoon raw cacao nibs)
- ¼ teaspoon ground cinnamon
- ¼ teaspoon ground chile powder

In small skillet over medium heat, toast sesame seeds until fragrant and lightly browned. Remove from heat and transfer to mortar. Add sea salt and grind until seeds start to break apart. Add remaining spices and seasonings accordingly. Grind to incorporate until seeds are about half ground. Serve as condiment or store in airtight container.

MAKES 2 tablespoons

SERVING SUGGESTION
I use the Toasted Nori and Garlic as an all-purpose seasoning blend, the Cumin Ginger on roasted cauliflower, legumes and sautéed greens, and the Cacao Chile to add zip to my steel-cut oats, lentil soup or roasted winter squash.

Spicy Aioli with Paprika

I USED TO THINK OF AIOLI STRICTLY AS A SUMMER DIP, until I made this warm and savory variation and tried it with steamed greens and chopped avocado. When I served it with a roasted portobello mushroom my family was convinced. And when I used it as a dip for sweet potato fries we became addicted.

---

3 garlic cloves, peeled

1 cup grapeseed oil mayonnaise

1 tablespoon lime juice

1 teaspoon paprika

1 tablespoon hot sauce of choice (we're fans of Cholula®)

¼ teaspoon cayenne

Pinch of sea salt

1 tablespoon chopped fresh cilantro

With food processor running, drop in garlic and process until minced. Turn food processor off and add mayonnaise, lime juice, paprika, hot sauce and cayenne. Process to combine. Add sea salt and cilantro and pulse to combine. Taste and adjust seasoning as desired. Remove from processor and serve or refrigerate in airtight container.

MAKES 1 cup

Not Your Store-Bought Ketchup

ONCE YOU'VE DISCOVERED THE AIOLI on the previous page, I'm not sure why you would need a recipe for ketchup. But just in case, here you go.

½ cup tomato paste

2 garlic cloves, finely minced

¼ cup chopped yellow onion

3 tablespoons maple syrup

2 tablespoons apple cider vinegar

½ teaspoon molasses

½ teaspoon mustard powder

½ teaspoon sea salt

Pinch of cayenne

1 tablespoon water, plus more to thin

In small pot over no heat, combine all ingredients. Turn heat to medium and cook, stirring continuously, for 3 minutes. Remove from heat and transfer to food processor. Purée until smooth and no pieces of garlic or onion are visible. Thin with more water as desired (ketchup will thicken once refrigerated) and transfer to a glass container. Refrigerate for at least 2 hours to allow flavors to blend before serving.

MAKES ¾ cup

Warm and Savory Roasted Squash Dip

LEFTOVER SQUASH INSPIRED THIS RECIPE. I wanted a snack that was warm and sweet and a finger food I could graze on. I reheated the previous night's roasted squash, added some spices, mashed it all together and enjoyed it with crackers. I call that upcycling at it's finest!

4	cups peeled and chopped butternut squash
4	shallots, peeled and quartered (about 1 cup)
2	tablespoons extra virgin olive oil
3	tablespoons whole coconut milk
¼	teaspoon freshly grated nutmeg
¼	teaspoon sea salt
⅛	teaspoon cayenne

Preheat oven to 400°F. Line a baking sheet with parchment paper.

Place squash and shallots in bowl, drizzle with olive oil and toss to evenly coat. Transfer to a baking sheet and arrange in a single layer. Roast 35 minutes or until squash is soft throughout and caramelized. Remove from oven and set aside to cool slightly.

Place roasted squash and shallots in food processor and process to combine. Add coconut milk, nutmeg, salt and cayenne and process to blend Adjust seasoning to taste with more salt and cayenne as desired. Process until smooth and serve warm.

MAKES 2 cups

Shiitake Mushroom and White Bean Dip

SAVORY, SALTY, RICH AND DECADENT…your guests will think you made this dip with heavy cream, but you'll know otherwise.

3 tablespoons extra virgin olive oil, plus more to taste

3 large shallots, finely chopped

½ pound shiitake mushrooms, stemmed and thinly sliced

4 garlic cloves, minced

1 tablespoon fresh thyme leaves

3 tablespoons Marsala cooking wine

1 cup cooked white beans (navy, great northern or cannellini)

¼ teaspoon sea salt

Lots of freshly ground pepper

In large cast iron skillet over medium-low heat, sauté shallots in olive oil until soft (about 3 minutes). Add mushrooms and continue sautéing, stirring as little as possible, to brown mushrooms (3–5 minutes). Stir in garlic and thyme. Add Marsala, 1 tablespoon at a time, to deglaze pan and infuse mushrooms with flavor. Increase heat to medium and sauté until mushrooms are well cooked and slightly caramelized (about 8 minutes total depending on how thinly they are sliced).

Fold in beans and continue sautéing until heated through. Add salt and season to taste with pepper. Remove from heat.

Transfer all ingredients to food processor and process until combined and mostly smooth with a few small chunks of mushroom remaining. Thin with extra virgin olive oil as desired. Serve warm, topped with a drizzle of olive oil.

MAKES 1½ cups

Red Onion Pomegranate Relish

ONE RECIPE—TWO GREAT RESULTS. Stop after the first paragraph of instructions and you'll have a delicious pomegranate molasses that can be used in marinades and dressings or drizzled over roasted vegetables and even desserts. Continue on to yield a delicious relish that complements everything from stuffed winter squash to your favorite pot pie.

1   cup 100% pomegranate juice

¼   cup maple syrup

Zest and juice of 1 lemon

2   tablespoons extra virgin olive oil

4   cups chopped red onion (about 4 large)

1   jalapeño, seeded and minced

Pinch of sea salt

In medium pot, combine pomegranate juice, maple syrup and lemon juice. Bring to a boil over high heat, reduce heat to medium-low and cook, stirring occasionally, until liquid reduces to about ½ cup and glazes the sides of the pot (about 1 hour). The mixture will thicken to molasses-like consistency as it cools. Remove from heat and set aside.

In cast iron skillet over medium heat, sauté onions in olive oil until soft and lightly browned (about 4 minutes). Add jalapeño to onion and continue sautéing 5 minutes longer. When onions and jalapeño are soft and browned, slowly stir in pomegranate syrup. Remove from heat, fold in lemon zest and sea salt and serve warm or at room temperature.

MAKES 1 cup

SERVING SUGGESTION
Serve pomegranate molasses drizzled over roasted roots and squashes, lentil dishes, soups, sliced oranges or nondairy ice cream! Will keep refrigerated in airtight container for weeks.

Basic Vegetable Stock

I GO TO THE FARM ON FRIDAY AFTERNOONS, so on Friday mornings I go through the refrigerator to see what vegetables remain. Uneaten vegetables from the previous week can be easily turned into vegetable stock. Every stock comes out differently as a result, but this is my basic formula.

---

1   tablespoon extra virgin olive oil

1   yellow onion, peeled and quartered

2   celery stalks, coarsely chopped

2   carrots, coarsely chopped

1   cup coarsely chopped green vegetables (broccoli, kale, collards…)

½   cup thinly sliced mushrooms (or ¼ cup dried mushrooms)

¼   cup fresh flat-leaf parsley (or 1 tablespoon dried)

2–3 sprigs fresh thyme (or 1 teaspoon dried)

1   teaspoon peppercorns

1   teaspoon sea salt

8   cups water

2   slices astragalus root (optional)

In large pot or Dutch oven, sauté onion, celery and carrots in olive oil until lightly browned (about 3 minutes). Add remaining ingredients, stir to combine and bring to boil. Reduce heat and simmer covered for 1 hour. Remove from heat and set aside to cool. Pour through mesh strainer into separate container, discard solid ingredients and refrigerate or freeze in airtight containers until ready to use.

MAKES 6 cups

Note: I use dried astragalus root to support immune strength and health in general by adding 1–2 slices to stocks, teas or anything that needs to steep for at least 20 minutes.

Red Lentil Curry Soup

I CAN'T EVEN THINK ABOUT EATING THIS SOUP without wanting to sit on the couch wrapped in a blanket. Guaranteed to warm your heart and soul on a cold day, this soup will have your kitchen smelling pretty fabulous, too!

1 tablespoon virgin coconut oil

1 large yellow onion, diced

3 celery stalks, chopped

1 red bell pepper, finely chopped

4 garlic cloves, minced

1 heaping tablespoon grated fresh ginger

1 heaping tablespoon grated fresh turmeric root (or 1 teaspoon ground)

1 heaping tablespoon curry powder

2 cups red lentils

6 cups vegetable stock

1½ cups whole coconut milk

1¼ teaspoons sea salt

1 cinnamon stick

2 tablespoons smooth peanut butter

2 tablespoons water

2 tablespoons lime juice

2 tablespoons chopped fresh cilantro

Melt coconut oil in large Dutch oven over medium heat. Add onion, celery and bell pepper and sauté 3 minutes. Add garlic, ginger, turmeric and curry powder and sauté 3 minutes longer.

Rinse lentils in a mesh strainer until water runs through clear. Add lentils to pot and fold to coat with spices. Add stock, coconut milk and sea salt and stir. Submerge cinnamon stick and bring soup to boil. Reduce heat and simmer with cover slightly ajar until lentils are soft and creamy (about 20 minutes). Remove from heat and remove and discard cinnamon stick. Whisk together peanut butter and water and stir into soup along with lime juice. Remove from heat and serve topped with cilantro.

SERVES 8

Sweet Potato Gumbo

I BROKE ALL THE RULES when I made this gumbo-style stew that warms my clearly not-so-Southern soul.

---

1   cup uncooked wild rice

3   cups water

3   cups peeled and cubed sweet potatoes

2   tablespoons extra virgin olive oil

1   large yellow onion, chopped

4   garlic cloves, minced

2   celery stalks, chopped

1   large green bell pepper, chopped

3   cups cooked kidney beans

1   tablespoon dried thyme

1   tablespoon paprika

½   teaspoon sea salt

¼   teaspoon freshly ground pepper

⅛   teaspoon cayenne

1½   cups diced tomatoes with their juices

2   tablespoons tomato paste

1   tablespoon red wine vinegar

4   cups vegetable stock

2   bay leaves

1   tablespoon arrowroot dissolved in 1 tablespoon water

6–8 dashes hot sauce

½   cup chopped scallions

Preheat oven to 400°F. Line a baking sheet with parchment paper.

Place wild rice and water in pot or rice cooker. Bring to boil, reduce heat and simmer covered until water is absorbed (about 40 minutes). Remove from heat and set aside to cool slightly. Fluff with wooden spoon when cool.

Meanwhile, place sweet potatoes in bowl, drizzle with 1 tablespoon olive oil and spread in single layer on prepared baking sheet. Roast 20 minutes or until caramelized and soft (time will vary depending on size of cubes). Remove from oven and set aside.

In large Dutch oven over high heat, brown onion, garlic, celery and bell pepper in remaining tablespoon olive oil until soft (3 minutes). Reduce heat to medium, add kidney beans, thyme, paprika, salt, pepper and cayenne and stir. Add tomatoes, tomato paste, vinegar and vegetable stock and stir to combine all ingredients. Submerge bay leaves and bring soup to boil. Reduce heat and simmer 30 minutes, stirring occasionally.

Add roasted sweet potatoes to soup and stir in dissolved arrowroot. Simmer 2 minutes longer, then remove from heat. Discard bay leaves and season with hot sauce.

Place a spoonful of wild rice in the center of each soup bowl, ladle gumbo around rice and serve topped with chopped scallions.

SERVES 8

Chinese Cabbage Soup

THIS RECIPE IS PROOF that cabbage is not an acceptable substitute for eggs (go figure), but you can't blame a girl for trying. I set out to make a vegan Egg Drop Soup and ended up creating something I love just as much. The taste is all its own, but the aroma is all egg drop soup (or perhaps I've just convinced myself because I wanted it to be).

8	cups vegetable stock
2	5-inch pieces of lemongrass
1	2-inch piece fresh ginger, peeled and thinly sliced
5	whole cloves
½	teaspoon black peppercorns
1	star anise
3	tablespoons tamari
6	cups thinly sliced napa cabbage
1	cup julienned snow peas
½	cup thinly sliced cremini mushroom caps
1	tablespoon arrowroot dissolved in 2 tablespoons cool water
3	tablespoons white miso (variety of choice) dissolved in 3 tablespoons cool water
4–6	dashes of hot pepper sesame oil
4	dashes of ume plum vinegar
½	cup chopped scallions

In Dutch oven, bring stock to simmer. Crush or twist lemongrass to release essence and add to stock along with ginger, cloves, peppercorns, star anise and tamari. Simmer 30 minutes and then scoop out and discard solids.

Stir in cabbage, snow peas and mushrooms and simmer until cabbage is wilted (about 5 minutes). Slowly pour in dissolved arrowroot and stir continuously for 1 minute longer. Remove from heat and stir in dissolved miso.

Drizzle with hot sesame oil and ume plum vinegar, top with scallions and serve hot.

SERVES 4

Ginger Lime Black Bean Soup with Mango

COLD WINTER DAYS are synonymous with hot soup. But even then, I crave the balance of refreshing raw fruits and vegetables. This soup delivers both and comes together in no time.

1½ cups dried black beans (4½ cups cooked)

1 thumb-size piece kombu

Pinch of sea salt

1 tablespoon extra virgin olive oil

1 large red onion, minced

4 garlic cloves, minced

1 heaping tablespoon grated fresh ginger

1 teaspoon ground cumin

3 cups vegetable stock, plus more to thin as desired

1 tablespoon lime juice

Sea salt and freshly ground pepper

TOPPING

½ cup chopped mango

½ cup chopped orange bell pepper

1 jalapeño, seeded and minced

¼ cup chopped fresh cilantro

2 teaspoons extra virgin olive oil

2 teaspoons lime juice

Pinch of sea salt

Place beans in pot, cover well with water and soak overnight.

Drain beans and rinse well. Bring pot of water to boil, add beans and cook 30 minutes. Remove from heat and drain cooking water. Return beans to stove and refill pot with enough water to cover by at least 2 inches. Submerge kombu, add salt and bring to boil. Reduce heat and simmer until beans are tender (about 45 minutes). Remove from heat, drain beans, discard kombu and set beans aside.

In Dutch oven over medium heat, sauté onion, garlic and ginger in olive oil until onion is lightly browned (about 4 minutes). Add cooked beans, cumin and stock and stir. Bring to boil, reduce heat and simmer 15 minutes. Remove from heat and use handheld blender to purée about half of mixture. Stir in lime juice and season to taste with salt and pepper. Return to heat and simmer 5 minutes longer. For thinner consistency, stir in additional vegetable stock ¼ cup at a time as desired.

Place all topping ingredients in small bowl and toss to combine.

Serve soup hot topped with a spoonful of mango-pepper mixture.

SERVES 4

Chopped Salad with Carrot Ginger Dressing

I ADORE THE SALAD DRESSING served by the Japanese restaurant down the street. It's cool and refreshing with just enough sweet and salt for balance, and even a hint of warming spice. I couldn't sleep until I figured out how to make it myself…and now you can be obsessed, too.

SALAD

1   head romaine lettuce, chopped

4–5 red leaf lettuce leaves, chopped

¼   cup peeled and julienned watermelon radish or daikon

¼   cup julienned carrot

DRESSING

2   carrots, chopped

1   small shallot, peeled

2   tablespoons grated fresh ginger

¼   cup extra virgin olive oil

3   tablespoons brown rice vinegar

1   tablespoon lime juice

1   tablespoon toasted sesame oil

¼   teaspoon hot pepper sesame oil

2   tablespoons white miso (variety of choice)

1   tablespoon mirin

Compose salad on individual plates with lettuces, radish and carrot.

In a food processor, combine carrots, shallot and ginger and pulse to chop. Add olive oil, rice vinegar, lime juice, both sesame oils, miso and mirin. Process to combine all ingredients and achieve blended dressing that is consistent but not completely smooth.

Spoon desired amount of dressing over each salad. Store leftover dressing refrigerated in airtight container.

SERVES 6 (makes 1½ cups dressing)

Avocado, Orange and Daikon Salad with Cumin Lime Vinaigrette

YOU COULD DRESS CARDBOARD WITH THIS VINAIGRETTE and I'd devour it, but you'll probably prefer this recipe featuring one of my favorite winter salad combinations. Sweet and juicy oranges, creamy rich avocado and pungent daikon make this a cleansing and refreshing raw winter salad.

VINAIGRETTE

- 3 tablespoons extra virgin olive oil
- 2 tablespoon lime juice
- 1 tablespoon maple syrup
- ½ teaspoon ground cumin

Sea salt and freshly ground pepper

SALAD

- 2 oranges
- ½ pomegranate
- ½ cup julienned daikon
- ½ cup peeled and julienned watermelon radish
- ½ medium red onion, thinly sliced
- 2 avocados, peeled, pitted and sliced into wedges
- ¼ cup toasted pine nuts

In small bowl, whisk together vinaigrette ingredients.

Cut skin and pith from orange and slice crosswise into thin rounds. Cut pomegranate in half. Hold one piece at a time, skin-side up, over a bowl. Slap the skin with the back of a wooden spoon to easily remove seeds. Add any pomegranate juice from bowl to vinaigrette and whisk to combine.

In large bowl, combine daikon, watermelon radish, red onion and orange rounds. Drizzle with all but 1 tablespoon vinaigrette and toss to coat and evenly distribute ingredients. Arrange on platter or individual plates. Place avocados in small bowl and drizzle with remaining dressing. Arrange on salad, top with pomegranate seeds and pine nuts and serve.

SERVES 6

VARIATION
Use 1 cup daikon radish if you are unable to find watermelon radishes, which can be elusive though well worth the hunt.

Mizuna Salad with Roasted Carrots and Asian Pears

WHEN THERE ARE NOT ENOUGH HOURS OF SUNLIGHT for hearty greens like kale and collards to grow, the greenhouses at the farm overflow with Asian greens, spinach and even arugula. Any can be used for this salad, but delicate and mustardy mizuna is my favorite…especially if you can find purple carrots to go with it.

4 medium carrots

1 teaspoon extra virgin olive oil

Pinch of sea salt

Pinch of ground cumin

Freshly ground pepper

2 cups mizuna greens

2 Asian pears, cored and thinly sliced

VINAIGRETTE

1 small shallot, minced

3 tablespoons extra virgin olive oil

1 tablespoon red wine vinegar

1 tablespoon maple syrup

Sea salt and freshly ground pepper

¼ cup chopped toasted pecans

Preheat oven to 425°F.

Cut carrots crosswise into 3- to 4-inch lengths, then halve or quarter lengthwise depending on size of carrots to yield equal-size sticks. Place in glass baking dish, drizzle with olive oil and sprinkle with salt, cumin and pepper to taste. Toss to evenly coat and roast 10 minutes. Remove from oven, toss to encourage even browning and return to oven to roast 10 minutes longer or until carrots are soft and starting to glaze (time will depend on size of carrots). Remove from oven and set aside.

Place greens on serving dish. When carrots are cool enough to touch, arrange with pear slices over mizuna.

In small skillet over medium-low heat, sauté shallot in 1 tablespoon olive oil until just soft (about 2 minutes). Remove from heat and stir in vinegar, maple syrup, remaining olive oil and salt and pepper to taste. Add toasted pecans and stir to coat. Drizzle over salad and serve.

SERVES 4

Arugula Salad with Creamy Lemon Parsley Dressing

THERE IS A GEM OF AN URBAN ORGANIC FARM not far from where I live where I get most of my produce. Each winter, one greenhouse in particular is dedicated to arugula. We call them virgin greens, as they've not been beaten by the weather. The hardest part about making this salad is keeping myself from eating all of the argula on the drive home!

---

6 cups loosely packed arugula

1 avocado, peeled and pitted

¼ cup juice-sweetened dried cranberries

¼ toasted pepitas (hulled pumpkin seeds)

DRESSING

1 garlic clove, peeled

2 tablespoons roasted tahini

Zest and juice of 1 lemon

3 tablespoons chopped fresh flat-leaf parsley

3 tablespoons extra virgin olive oil

⅛ teaspoon sea salt

3 tablespoons water

Place arugula in salad bowl. Slice avocado into wedges and place on salad. Sprinkle on cranberries and pepitas and set aside.

In small bowl, place all dressing ingredients except water and use handheld blender to process until combined. Add water 1 tablespoon at a time and process until smooth.

Drizzle desired amount of dressing over salad and serve. Store remaining dressing refrigerated in airtight container.

SERVES 4 (makes ⅔ cup dressing)

Collard Green Maki with Sesame Dipping Sauce

SOMETIMES COLLARD GREENS ARE SO BIG and beautiful that it's a shame to chop them up. In this recipe, the collards serve as the wrap and make this handroll especially nutritious and delicious.

DIPPING SAUCE

- 3 tablespoons tamari
- 1 teaspoon grated fresh ginger
- 1 teaspoon toasted or hot pepper sesame oil
- 1 teaspoon brown rice vinegar
- 1 teaspoon toasted sesame seeds

HANDROLL

- 1 cup uncooked short-grain brown rice
- 2 cups water
- 1 thumb-size piece kombu
- 6 large collard greens
- 1 large leek, halved lengthwise and cut crosswise into ½-inch half-moons
- 2 cups thinly sliced shiitake mushroom caps
- 1 tablespoon extra virgin olive oil
- 1 tablespoon tamari
- 1 cup julienned carrots
- 1 cup julienned daikon
- 1 avocado, peeled, pitted and sliced

In small bowl, whisk together all dipping sauce ingredients and set aside.

Place rice, water and kombu in medium pot or rice cooker. Bring to boil, reduce heat and simmer covered until liquid is absorbed (about 30 minutes). Remove from heat and set aside. When cool, remove and discard kombu.

In medium pot, bring 3 inches water to boil. Turn off heat and one at a time, holding the collard leaves by their stems, submerge leaves in water for 3–5 seconds each (or until just bright green). Repeat until all greens are lightly blanched and set aside.

In large cast iron skillet over medium heat, sauté leek and shiitakes in olive oil until soft (about 5 minutes). Add tamari and stir. Add carrots and daikon and continue sautéing. If ingredients stick, deglaze pan by adding 1 tablespoon water at a time as needed. When carrots are just soft and bright orange, remove from heat and set aside.

Place one collard green on cutting board, spread a heaping tablespoon of brown rice crosswise across the widest part of the leaf leaving 1 inch clean along each edge. Top with a small scoop of mushroom mixture and then with a slice of avocado. Fold insides of collard leaf and roll, starting at the end with the rice and vegetables to form a log. Continue with remaining ingredients until everything is used up.

Cut rolls in half and serve with dipping sauce.

MAKES 6 rolls

Fingerling Potatoes and Brussels Sprouts with Horseradish Dressing

I COULD EAT "ALL THE COLORS OF THE RAINBOW" just by eating fingerling potatoes, but I don't want to see what I'd look like (or how I'd feel) if I did. The deep purple fingerlings are my all-time favorites, but any color or combination will work fine in this recipe.

DRESSING

2   tablespoons grapeseed oil mayonnaise

1   avocado, peeled and pitted

3   tablespoons peeled and grated fresh horseradish

1   teaspoon maple or Dijon mustard

1   tablespoon lemon juice

¼   cup extra virgin olive oil

1   tablespoon chopped fresh parsley

Sea salt and freshly ground pepper

VEGETABLES

1   pound fingerling potatoes (any variety or color)

1   pound Brussels sprouts, trimmed

1   tablespoon extra virgin olive oil

1   teaspoon coarse sea salt

PREPARING DRESSING

In small bowl, mash together mayonnaise, avocado, horseradish, mustard and lemon juice until mostly smooth. Add olive oil and whisk to combine well. Fold in parsley and season to taste with sea salt and pepper. Refrigerate in airtight container at least 3 hours to allow flavors to develop.

PREPARING VEGETABLES

Preheat oven to 400°F.

Scrub potatoes, cut lengthwise into halves or quarters (depending on size of potatoes) to yield similar-size pieces, and place in bowl. Halve or quarter Brussels sprouts similarly. Drizzle with olive oil, sprinkle with sea salt and spread in single layer on baking sheet. Place in oven and roast 30 minutes or until potatoes are soft, checking frequently to toss and encourage even roasting.

Serve vegetables either tossed with dressing or with dressing as dipping sauce on the side.

SERVES 4

Sautéed Kale with Tahini Miso Dressing

WHEN I FIRST STARTED TEACHING COOKING CLASSES, nobody knew what kale was. Today, this dark leafy green has come into its own. Because kale loves the cold, we enjoy its health benefits all winter long, sometimes even pushing aside snow in our garden to pick a few leaves.

DRESSING

1   tablespoons roasted tahini
1   tablespoons lemon juice
1   tablespoon white miso (variety of choice)
1   tablespoon maple syrup
1   tablespoon water

KALE

1   tablespoon extra virgin olive oil
½   small red onion, cut into thin wedges
2   bunches kale, chopped
1   avocado, peeled, pitted and chopped

In small bowl, whisk together all dressing ingredients and set aside.

In cast iron skillet or Dutch oven over medium heat, sauté onion in olive oil until soft (about 3 minutes). Add kale and fold continuously until wilted and dark green. Pour dressing over kale, fold to combine and remove from heat. Top with chopped avocado and serve warm.

SERVES 6

Sweet and Smokey Brussels Sprouts

I WOULDN'T TOUCH A BRUSSELS SPROUT until I was an adult. Now I eat them so much I can barely remember those boiled mushy sprouts of my youth…much. Pan-seared or roasted with just a little bit of garlic, olive oil and sea salt were my perennial favorite preparations, until I came up with this combination.

Zest of 1 lemon plus
    1 tablespoon juice

1 tablespoon mirin

1 tablespoon maple syrup

½ teaspoon mustard powder

¼ teaspoon paprika

1 pound Brussels sprouts

2 tablespoons extra virgin olive oil

½ teaspoon coarse sea salt

In small bowl, whisk together lemon juice, mirin, maple syrup, mustard and paprika.

Trim Brussels sprouts by cutting off dry root ends and peeling away damaged leaves. Cut into halves, quarters or wedges (depending on size of sprouts) to yield pieces of similar size.

Heat cast iron skillet over medium-high heat and add olive oil. Add sprouts, stir continuously and sauté until evenly seared and just soft (about 4 minutes). Add lemon mixture and sauté 2 minutes longer to glaze.

Remove from heat, toss with lemon zest and coarse sea salt and serve.

SERVES 4

Roasted Fennel and Multicolored Beets

THIS IS ONE OF THOSE MELT-IN-YOUR-MOUTH side dishes that can turn a simple meal into something special. I like to serve this alongside a roasted portobello mushroom with some simple black lentils.

3 medium beets (any color or variety)

1 large fennel bulb

1 teaspoon extra virgin olive oil

DRESSING

1 tablespoon extra virgin olive oil

2 teaspoons golden or white balsamic vinegar

Pinch of dried thyme or lemon thyme

Sea salt and freshly ground pepper

Preheat oven to 400°F.

Scrub and trim beets. Wrap in loose foil pouch, place pouch on glass baking dish (to catch drips) and roast for 50 minutes or until cooked through (time will vary depending on size of beets).

After beets have roasted 30 minutes, prepare fennel by removing and discarding dried root end and stalks. Slice bulb into thin wedges through core (keeping core intact to hold wedges together). Toss with olive oil, wrap in separate foil pouch and add to oven to roast along with beets. When fennel is soft (about 15 minutes), open foil around fennel and roast 5 minutes longer or until soft and just browned. Remove beets and fennel from oven.

When beets are cool enough to touch, peel by pushing away skins with thumbs. Slice beets into wedges and place in glass baking dish. Add fennel and set aside.

Pour juice from roasting beets into small bowl. Add all dressing ingredients to same bowl and whisk together. Drizzle over beets and fennel, toss to coat and serve warm.

SERVES 4

Acorn Squash Cups with Ginger Apple Stuffing

CARAMELIZED ROASTED SQUASH with sweet and savory fruit stuffing make this a satisfying and warming side dish that you may just want to eat for breakfast (or even dessert).

2	small acorn squash
1	tablespoon virgin coconut oil
½	cup chopped red onion
½	cup chopped celery
1	heaping tablespoon grated fresh ginger
2	tart red apples, chopped
½	cup raisins
¼	heaping teaspoon ground cinnamon
3	tablespoons maple syrup

Preheat oven to 400°F. Line a baking sheet with parchment paper.

Cut squash in half crosswise. Scoop out and discard seeds and trim off stems and pointed ends so they sit flat. Place skin-side up on prepared baking sheet and roast 30 minutes or until soft (time will depend on size of squash). Remove from oven and set aside.

Melt coconut oil in cast iron skillet over medium-low heat. Add onion, celery, ginger and apples and sauté until just soft (about 3 minutes). Add raisins, cinnamon and maple syrup and sauté until just soft and caramelized (about 3 minutes longer). Remove from heat, fill each squash half with an equal amount of stuffing and serve.

SERVES 4

Orange Roasted Broccoli

THIS IS THE FIRST HEALTHY LUNCH RECIPE we introduced at the local upper elementary school. It's quick, easy and was an instant success. When I made it for dinner that night, my girls exclaimed, "Hey look, Mom made cafeteria food for dinner!" Tough crowd.

4   medium heads broccoli, chopped into similar-size pieces

3   tablespoons extra virgin olive oil

½   teaspoon coarse sea salt

Freshly ground pepper

Zest and juice of 1 orange

Preheat oven to 425°F.

Place broccoli in large bowl, drizzle with olive oil and toss to coat. Sprinkle on sea salt and a generous amount of pepper and toss to combine all ingredients. Transfer to glass baking dish and roast 15 minutes or until lightly browned on outside and tender when pricked with fork (time will depend on size of broccoli pieces).

Remove from oven, drizzle orange juice evenly over broccoli and add orange zest. Fold to combine all ingredients and serve.

SERVES 4

Caramelized Delicata Squash with Shallots and Currants

YOU CAN'T KNOCK A SQUASH that's easy to grow, sweet and delicious, and doesn't require peeling or weightlifting in order to chop (no disrespect intended to butternut and kabocha).

---

2   medium delicata squash
2   tablespoons extra virgin olive oil
1   tablespoon maple syrup
4   shallots, sliced into thin rings
2   tablespoons dried currants
⅛   teaspoon freshly grated nutmeg
Sea salt and freshly ground pepper

Cut squash in half lengthwise. Scoop out and discard seeds and cut crosswise into ½-inch slices. Heat large cast iron skillet over medium heat and coat bottom with 1 tablespoon olive oil. Place squash in pan and sauté until evenly seared (about 1 minute per side). Drizzle maple syrup evenly over squash and continue sautéing until caramelized. Transfer from pan to serving dish and set aside.

Add remaining 1 tablespoon olive oil to pan and sauté shallot for 2 minutes. Add currants and nutmeg and sauté until shallots start to brown (2 minutes longer). Season to taste with salt and pepper. Remove from heat, spoon over arranged squash and serve.

SERVES 4

Vegetable Curry Pot Pie

I RARELY TAKE THE TIME TO MAKE POT PIE in its truest form.
In fact, any combination of vegetables in a pot with something crust-like
over it saves me time and effort and scores points with my family.

CRUST

1	cup brown rice flour
½	cup tapioca flour/starch
2	teaspoons baking powder
1	teaspoon sea salt
4	tablespoons virgin coconut oil
½	cup rice or almond milk
1	tablespoon lemon juice

FILLING

1	tablespoon extra virgin olive oil
1	yellow onion, chopped
3	garlic cloves, minced
1	tablespoon grated fresh turmeric root (or 1 teaspoon ground)
3	celery stalks, chopped
2	cups chopped carrots
4	cups chopped cauliflower
2	tablespoons mirin
2	large bunches Swiss chard, chopped

2 cups peas, fresh or frozen

Sea salt and freshly ground pepper

1½ cups vegetable stock

2 tablespoons arrowroot

1½ teaspoons curry powder

Preheat oven to 400°F.

Place crust ingredients in refrigerator to chill.

In large Dutch oven over medium heat, sauté onion and garlic in olive oil until soft (about 3 minutes). Stir in turmeric, celery, carrots and cauliflower. Add mirin, stir and simmer 2 minutes. Add Swiss chard and peas and fold continuously until chard wilts. Season to taste with sea salt and pepper. In a bowl, whisk together vegetable stock, arrowroot and curry powder. Pour into vegetable mixture and stir until sauce thickens (1–2 minutes). Remove from heat and set aside.

In food processor, combine chilled brown rice flour, tapioca flour, baking powder and sea salt and pulse to combine. Add coconut oil 1 tablespoon at a time and pulse to cut into flour mixture. In small bowl, combine milk and lemon juice. With food processor running, pour in milk mixture. Process until just combined. Place a sheet of parchment paper on cutting board and transfer dough to paper. Form into ball and then press into round to fit your Dutch oven (about ½-inch thick).

Place dough round over vegetables in Dutch oven and bake 35 minutes or until vegetables are soft and filling is bubbling up over crust. Remove from heat and set aside 2–3 minutes to cool before serving.

SERVES 6

Roasted Cauliflower with Turmeric

THIS BECAME A MUST-HAVE WINTER STAPLE in my kitchen after I made the Cauliflower Steak recipe *(page 191)*. I had all those leftover florets, so I prepared them as described below and they disappeared within minutes of coming out of the oven. Now I buy cauliflower just to make these, and we still eat them straight off the pan!

2   heads cauliflower (about 8 cups chopped)

3   tablespoons extra virgin olive oil

2   tablespoons ground turmeric

1   tablespoon paprika

½   teaspoon coarse sea salt

Preheat oven to 400°F.

Slice heads of cauliflower in half and then in quarters. Cut the stem on the diagonal to remove and discard. Break or cut tops into florets of a similar size. In large bowl, toss florets with olive oil. Sprinkle with turmeric, paprika and sea salt, toss and spread into a single layer over 2 baking sheets.

Place in oven and roast 15 minutes. Remove from oven, flip florets so they roast evenly and return to oven to roast 15 minutes longer or until golden and soft.

Remove from oven and serve (or simply eat off the pan).

SERVES 6

Roasted Roots and Blood Oranges with Millet

MILLET'S NUTTY TASTE complements everything from dark leafy greens to sweet winter squash to legumes. But it's the roasted blood oranges that make this dish so much more than just a winter staple.

½ cup uncooked millet

1 cup water

Pinch of sea salt

2 blood oranges

6 cups peeled and diced root vegetables (carrot, parsnip, rutabaga, turnip...)

¼ fennel bulb, cored and sliced into thin wedges

2 tablespoons extra virgin olive oil

1 teaspoon coarse sea salt

½ cup coarsely chopped toasted pecans

¼ cup chopped juice-sweetened dried cherries

1 tablespoon chopped fresh flat-leaf parsley

DRESSING

2 tablespoons extra virgin olive oil

1 tablespoon orange juice

1 tablespoon lemon juice

1 tablespoon maple syrup

1 teaspoon orange zest

½ teaspoon mustard powder

Sea salt and freshly ground pepper

Preheat oven to 425°F.

Rinse millet in mesh strainer and drain well. Heat Dutch oven or skillet with lid over medium-high heat. Add millet and pan toast until dry and fragrant (about 2 minutes). Add water and salt, reduce heat to low and simmer covered until liquid is absorbed (about 25 minutes). Remove from heat and set aside to cool at least 5 minutes.

Slice unpeeled oranges into ¼-inch rounds. Place in two 9 x 12-inch baking dishes along with root vegetables and fennel. Drizzle with olive oil, sprinkle with sea salt and toss to coat. Place in oven and roast 30 minutes or until vegetables are soft and slightly browned (tossing vegetables and flipping oranges every 10 minutes). Remove from oven and set aside.

Fluff millet with wooden spoon and fold in roasted vegetables, pecans and cherries.

In small bowl, whisk together olive oil, orange juice, lemon juice, maple syrup, orange zest, mustard and plenty of salt and pepper. Drizzle over millet and fold to combine. Top with roasted roots and oranges, garnish with parsley and serve.

SERVES 6

Baked Macaroni and Cheese with Peas and Chard

I'VE MADE MAC AND CHEESE FOR MY KIDS more times than I can count. For years I had Annie's Organic to thank, but now I go with this homemade variation and make my own "cheese." I insist that we have to add something green, and peas and chard are always my girls' top choice.

2½ cups peeled and cubed butternut squash (about ½ small squash)

⅔ cup rice milk or water

3 tablespoons nutritional yeast

3 tablespoons chickpea miso

½ teaspoon garlic powder

½ teaspoon sea salt

Generous pinch of freshly grated nutmeg

8 ounces gluten-free macaroni

1 cup peas, fresh or frozen

1 cup chopped green Swiss chard

½ cup gluten-free bread or rice crumbs

1 tablespoon extra virgin olive oil, plus more for oiling baking dish

Paprika

Bring 1 inch of water to boil in medium pot with steamer rack. Add squash and steam until very soft.

Transfer squash to food processor. Add rice milk, nutritional yeast, miso, garlic powder, salt and nutmeg and process until combined and smooth. Turn processor off, scrape down sides and pulse one last time to combine all ingredients. Set aside.

Preheat oven to 350°F. Lightly oil an 8 x 8-inch baking dish.

Cook macaroni according to directions on package. When nearly done, add peas and chard to cooking water with macaroni and remove from heat. Drain and return to pot. Pour squash mixture into pot and fold to evenly coat pasta and vegetables. Transfer to baking dish and spread evenly.

In small bowl, combine breadcrumbs with olive oil and mix until moist. Spread over casserole, sprinkle with paprika and bake 30 minutes, or until breadcrumbs are lightly toasted. Remove from oven and serve.

SERVES 6

Basmati Rice with French Lentils and Fennel

LOOKING FOR A QUICK AND EASY DINNER? This recipe is it. High-protein lentils, soothing fennel and all-purpose ume vinegar come together to make a base for everything from roasted vegetables to sautéed greens to pan-seared tempeh (or all of them together).

¾ cup uncooked brown basmati rice

½ cup French lentils

2½ cups water

Pinch of sea salt

1 tablespoon extra virgin olive oil, plus more for drizzling

1 red onion, chopped

1 small fennel bulb, cored and finely chopped

1 teaspoon minced fresh rosemary

3–5 dashes of ume plum vinegar

¼ cup chopped fresh cilantro or flat-leaf parsley

Rinse rice and lentils in mesh strainer and drain. Place in rice cooker or Dutch oven with water and sea salt and bring to boil. Reduce heat and simmer covered until liquid is absorbed (about 35 minutes). Remove from heat and set aside to cool slightly.

In cast iron skillet over medium heat, sauté onion and fennel in olive oil until soft (about 3 minutes). Add rosemary and sauté 1 minute longer. Remove from heat.

Fluff rice-lentil mixture and fold in onion mixture. Season with ume plum vinegar and an extra drizzle of olive oil. Toss with chopped cilantro and serve.

SERVES 6

Amaranth Falafel Patties

THEY MAKE A KILLER FALAFEL at Tangiers Market in West Hartford. I imagine that their success comes, in part, from their pot covered with decades of seasoning. Since they're not giving up their pot, I've taken a completely different approach with this recipe.

DRESSING

2	garlic cloves, peeled
1	avocado, peeled and pitted
½	cup tahini
3	tablespoons lemon juice
¼	teaspoon sea salt
¼	cup warm water (or amount as needed)

FALAFEL

1	tablespoon grapeseed or extra virgin olive oil
1	yellow onion, minced
3	garlic cloves, minced
1	teaspoon ground cumin
½	teaspoon ground coriander
½	teaspoon sea salt
¼	teaspoon freshly ground pepper
3	dashes of cayenne
¾	cup uncooked amaranth
1½	cups vegetable stock
¼	cup gluten-free breadcrumbs (or amount as needed)

With food processor running, drop in garlic to mince. Turn processor off and add avocado, tahini, lemon juice and salt and process until smooth. Pour in water slowly (amount needed will depend on thickness of tahini) and process until smooth and creamy like salad dressing. Set aside.

In Dutch oven over medium-high heat, sear onion and garlic in oil until lightly browned. Stir in cumin, coriander, salt, pepper and cayenne. Add amaranth and stock and bring to boil. Reduce heat and simmer covered until liquid is absorbed (about 45 minutes). Remove from heat and set aside to cool and firm for 10 minutes.

Preheat oven to 350°F. Line a baking sheet with parchment paper.

Fold breadcrumbs into amaranth 1 tablespoon at a time until mixture resembles stiff cookie dough. You may not need all of the breadcrumbs (amount will depend on how long batter has set). Scoop dough into 8 portions (about 1 heaping tablespoon each) and form into balls. Place on prepared baking sheet and press down gently to form round patties 2½ inches in diameter and ¾-inch thick.

Bake patties 12 minutes on each side, remove from oven and serve with a dollop of dressing.

SERVES 4 (makes 8 patties)

Creamy Lentil Vegetable Casserole

A HEARTY ONE-POT MEAL LIKE THIS ONE, that satisfies my whole family and can be made ahead of time, is a guaranteed winner.

1½ cups black lentils
2¼ cups water
Pinch of sea salt
2 tablespoons extra virgin olive oil
1 medium onion, diced
3 carrots, thinly sliced
1 bunch kale, chopped
3 cups chopped cauliflower

SAUCE

2 cups vegetable stock
2 cups chopped cauliflower
1 cup nutritional yeast
¼ teaspoon mustard powder
1 tablespoon arrowroot
Sea salt and freshly ground pepper

CRUMB TOPPING

½ cup gluten-free bread crumbs
1 teaspoons dried parsley
½ teaspoon dried thyme
¼ teaspoon celery seed
2 tablespoons extra virgin olive oil
Paprika

Rinse lentils in a mesh strainer and drain. Place in pot or rice cooker with water and a pinch of sea salt. Bring to boil, reduce heat and simmer covered until liquid is absorbed (about 15 minutes). Remove from heat and set aside.

Preheat oven to 350°F.

In large Dutch oven over medium heat, sauté onion in olive oil until soft (about 3 minutes). Add carrots, kale and cauliflower and sauté until just soft (about 3 minutes longer). Fold in lentils and continue sautéing to heat through. Remove from heat, cover and set aside.

In medium pot over high heat, bring stock to boil. Reduce heat, add cauliflower and simmer until soft (about 5 minutes). Add nutritional yeast, mustard and arrowroot. Remove from heat and purée with handheld blender until smooth. Season to taste with salt and pepper.

Pour sauce over lentil-vegetable mixture and gently press it into the casserole so that sauce seeps down into lentils and veggies.

In small bowl, combine breadcrumbs, parsley, thyme and celery seed. Drizzle with olive oil and stir to combine so crumbs are evenly moist. Sprinkle over top of casserole and gently press into sauce. Sprinkle with paprika.

Bake uncovered for 20 minutes (or until bubbling on sides and lightly browned on top). Remove from heat and serve.

SERVES 6

Tamarind and Blood Orange Tofu

THE BRIDGE BRAND TOFU IS SO DELICIOUS I could eat it straight from the package. Their process is slow and by hand, their soybeans are organic and locally grown and it's all been that way from the start over 25 years ago. I realize that for most, tofu isn't exactly a splurge, but for me, this locally produced tofu is just that.

½ cup blood orange juice

1 teaspoon tamarind paste

2 tablespoons maple syrup

½ teaspoon five-spice powder

Pinch of sea salt

2 pounds fresh tofu (not silken)

1 tablespoon extra virgin olive oil

1 bunch scallions, chopped

In small bowl, whisk together blood orange juice, tamarind paste, maple syrup, five-spice powder and sea salt.

Slice tofu into ½-inch-thick slices. Heat olive oil in large cast iron skillet over medium-high heat. Add tofu and sauté 2 minutes on each side or until lightly browned and crisp. Drizzle orange-tamarind mixture evenly over tofu slices and slide pan back and forth over burner to evenly distribute. When mixture starts to thicken and glaze tofu, flip slices and continue sautéing, being sure not to let glaze burn. When tofu slices are browned and well glazed, remove from heat.

Transfer tofu to serving tray and drizzle with glaze remaining in pan. Set aside for 2–3 minutes to allow tofu to firm. Top with chopped scallions and serve.

SERVES 6

SERVING SUGGESTION
Toss sautéed tofu with baby broccoli and serve over buckwheat noodles dressed with toasted sesame oil and ume plum vinegar.

Stuffed Butternut Squash with Tempeh

I USUALLY LOOK FOR BUTTERNUT SQUASH with a long neck and a small bulb so that I get the most squash and the least amount of seeds. For this recipe, I want the opposite—a larger cavity for filling and just a little squash to add to my stuffing.

¼   cup uncooked wild rice

¼   cup uncooked brown basmati rice

1½ cups water or vegetable stock

Pinch of sea salt

1   large butternut squash

2   tablespoons plus ½ teaspoon extra virgin olive oil

2   shallots, chopped

3   garlic cloves, minced

1   celery stalk, finely chopped

8   ounces tempeh

2   tablespoons lemon juice

2   tablespoons maple syrup

Pinch of red pepper flakes

2   tablespoons chopped fresh flat-leaf parsley

Seeds from ½ pomegranate

Preheat oven to 425°F. Line 2 baking sheets with parchment paper.

Place wild and basmati rice in pot or rice cooker with water or stock and a pinch of sea salt. Bring to boil, reduce heat and simmer covered until liquid is absorbed (about 45 minutes). Remove from heat and set aside.

Cut squash lengthwise so that you have one piece that is more than half (about two-thirds) and the other about one-third. Scoop out and discard seeds, and rub larger piece with ½ teaspoon olive oil. Place flesh-side down on prepared baking sheet. Peel other piece and cut into ½-inch cubes. Place cubes in bowl, toss with 1 tablespoon olive oil and spread in single layer on second baking sheet. Roast both 35 minutes or until tender. Remove from oven and set aside.

In cast iron skillet over medium heat, sauté shallots and garlic in remaining 1 tablespoon olive oil until soft (about 2 minutes). Add celery and sauté 2 minutes longer. Crumble tempeh and add to pan. In bowl, combine lemon juice and maple syrup and pour over tempeh. Fold to combine and continue sautéing to heat through.

Fluff grain and add to tempeh mixture. Fold in pepper flakes, cubed squash and parsley. Scoop out the roasted squash leaving ½-inch of squash plus shell. Fill squash with stuffing allowing it to overflow generously. Top with pomegranate seeds, slice into 4 equal portions and serve.

SERVES 4

Mung Bean Stew

TRADITIONALLY KNOWN AS KITCHARI, this Ayurvedic stew is used for detoxing and balancing one's constitution. Mung beans are high in protein and fiber making this a healing and comforting one-pot meal.

1	cup mung beans
2	tablespoons virgin coconut oil
1	teaspoon mustard seeds
1	teaspoon cumin seeds
1	teaspoon fennel seeds
1	tablespoon grated fresh ginger
1	tablespoon grated fresh turmeric root (or 1 teaspoon ground)
1	cup uncooked basmati rice
1	medium yam, unpeeled and chopped
2	carrots, unpeeled and chopped
2	cups chopped cauliflower
4½	cups water or vegetable stock
2	cinnamon sticks
1	thumb-size piece kombu soaked in ½ cup water
½	teaspoon sea salt
¼	cup chopped fresh cilantro

Place mung beans in pot, cover well with water and soak overnight. Drain soaking water, rinse and drain beans, and set aside.

Melt coconut oil in Dutch oven over low heat. Add mustard, cumin and fennel seeds and toast 2 minutes or until fragrant. Add ginger and turmeric and sauté 2 minutes longer. Add mung beans and rice and fold to evenly coat with seeds and spices. Add yam, carrots and cauliflower. Pour in water and submerge cinnamon sticks. Remove kombu from soaking water and mince. Add to pot along with soaking water. Increase heat to high and bring to boil. Reduce heat and simmer covered until consistency is that of a thick stew (about 50 minutes). Remove from heat and discard cinnamon sticks. Stir in sea salt and cilantro and serve.

Note: Avoid overseasoning as kitchari is intended to be gentle.

SERVES 8

VARIATION
I use coconut oil, but ghee is traditionally used and imparts significant health benefits. Vegetable ghee does exist, but is not readily available in many areas.

Chocolate Almond Biscotti

THESE BISCOTTI ARE FRAGILE "IN THE MAKE," but will be well worth the delicate hand once they're done!

DRY INGREDIENTS

1½ cups almond flour/meal

1 cup teff flour
(ivory or brown)

¼ cup tapioca flour/starch

2 tablespoons cacao powder

1 tablespoon baking powder

½ teaspoon ground cinnamon

½ teaspoon sea salt

WET INGREDIENTS

¼ cup virgin coconut oil, melted

½ cup maple syrup

¼ cup coconut nectar

1 teaspoon vanilla extract

1 teaspoon almond extract

¼ cup applesauce

Preheat oven to 350°F. Line 2 baking sheets with parchment paper.

In medium bowl, whisk together all dry ingredients. In separate bowl, mix together all wet ingredients. Pour the wet ingredients into the dry and stir or fold gently to combine. Divide batter in half, scoop each half onto a baking sheet to form a long thin log (about 3 inches wide). Bake for 20 minutes.

Remove from oven and cool for 10 minutes. Reduce oven to 300°F. Use a serrated knife to carefully slice log on the diagonal into 1-inch pieces (clean knife between cuts if batter sticks). Slide knife under each piece to lift and turn it onto its side. Bake 15 minutes. Remove from heat, flip cookies to other side and bake 15 minutes longer. Remove from heat and set aside to cool completely before serving or storing.

MAKES 16 biscotti

Peppermint Slice

THE REQUEST FOR THIS RECIPE came via email from Australia. "Please clean up my husband's favorite holiday dessert" it said. I quickly learned that Peppermint Slice is traditional Down Under, but its chocolate biscuit, peppermint icing and chocolate topping are anything but clean...until now. Enjoy mates!

BASE

2	cups pecans
1	cup brown rice flour
¼	cup cacao powder
¼	teaspoon sea salt
⅓	cup virgin coconut oil, melted
⅓	cup maple syrup

ICING

½	cup whole coconut milk
1	teaspoon coconut oil
½	teaspoon vanilla extract
½	teaspoon peppermint extract
2	teaspoons coconut syrup or brown rice syrup
1	teaspoon arrowroot

TOPPING

6	ounces dark chocolate (70% cacao or more)
¼	teaspoon virgin coconut oil
¼	teaspoon coarse sea salt

Preheat oven to 350°F. Line an 8 x 8-inch baking dish with parchment paper, with overlap on two sides.

In a food processor, combine pecans, rice flour, cacao and salt and pulse to make a crumb-like mixture. Add coconut oil and maple syrup and process to form a moist ball. Place ball in prepared baking dish and press over bottom to form base. Bake 20 minutes or until top appears dry. Remove from oven and set on wire rack to cool completely.

In small pan over no heat, combine coconut milk, coconut oil, extracts, and coconut syrup. Whisk in arrowroot, turn heat to medium and whisk continuously until icing thickens. Remove from heat, spread evenly over pecan base and refrigerate.

In small pot over low heat, combine chocolate and coconut oil. Stir continuously until chocolate is melted and smooth and oil is blended in. Remove base from refrigerator and pour chocolate evenly over peppermint filling. Tilt the baking dish in each direction so that melted chocolate evenly covers the top. Sprinkle with coarse sea salt and refrigerate until topping is firm.

Remove from refrigerator 30 minutes prior to serving. Lift dessert out of baking dish by pulling up paper. Gently cut dessert into 25 squares, about 1½ x 1½ inches each, and serve.

MAKES 25 bars

Pecan Cutout Cookies

THIS RECIPE IS ADAPTED FROM ONE OF THE TARTS in my first cookbook. I had just started making the tart when I realized that the crust would work perfectly for cutout cookies. I scratched the tart, made the cookies instead and now turn to this recipe every holiday season.

2 cups pecans

1 cup brown rice flour

¼ cup virgin coconut oil, melted

¼ cup maple syrup

Maple sugar or coconut palm sugar for garnish

Preheat oven to 350°F. Line a baking sheet with parchment paper.

Place pecans in food processor and process to coarsely chop. Add brown rice flour and pulse briefly. In small bowl, combine oil and syrup, add to nut mixture and process until combined.

Transfer dough to parchment-lined surface and press or roll dough out to ¼-inch thickness. Cut with cookie cutters of choice and place cookies on baking sheet. Press dough scraps into a ball and roll out again to make more cookies. Repeat to use up all dough.

Sprinkle cookies with maple sugar or coconut palm sugar and bake 15 minutes or until golden brown. Remove from oven and set on wire rack to cool.

MAKES about two dozen 2-inch cutout cookies

VARIATION
Top cookies with frosting used for Carrot Cake *(page 80)*.

Congo Bars

DECADENT CHOCOLATE, NUTS AND COCONUT with just enough flour to hold it all together—that's what I call a perfect dessert!

¼ teaspoon virgin coconut oil, plus more for greasing pan

1 cup ivory teff flour

1 cup almond flour/meal

2 teaspoons baking powder

½ teaspoon sea salt

¼ cup plus 2 tablespoons applesauce

1 cup maple syrup

½ cup cashew butter

2 teaspoons vanilla extract

½ cup chopped pecans

½ cup unsweetened dried shredded coconut

½ cup dark chocolate chunks

Preheat oven to 350°F. Grease an 8 x 8-inch glass baking dish with coconut oil.

In large bowl, combine teff flour, almond flour, baking powder and salt. In separate bowl, whisk together applesauce, maple syrup, cashew butter and vanilla. Pour wet ingredients into dry and fold until just combined. Fold in pecans and coconut, transfer batter to prepared baking dish and spread evenly. Use a table knife to draw four evenly spaced parallel "channels" across the batter.

In small pot over medium-low heat, melt coconut oil and chocolate chunks. Stir until combined and smooth. Remove from heat and pour chocolate evenly into channels. Drag table knife across the channels of chocolate, perpendicular to the channels and going first one direction, then back again, to create a swirling pattern. Bake for 35 minutes or until a toothpick inserted in center comes out clean.

Set aside to cool and set. Cut into 16 bars, delicately remove from pan and serve.

MAKES 16 bars

NoNo Bars

MY DAUGHTER SARAH NAMED THESE BARS because there's nothing to them. No grain, no nuts, no baking, no fuss! There's lots of room to play in this recipe as long as you stick to 4 cups of dry ingredients to 1 cup of wet ingredients.

---

1   cup unsweetened dried shredded coconut

1   cup sprouted or toasted pumpkin seeds

1   cup sprouted or toasted sunflower seeds

½   cup juice-sweetened dried cranberries

½   cup raisins

3   tablespoons cacao nibs

½   cup sunflower butter

½   cup coconut nectar

Pinch of sea salt

In large bowl, combine coconut, pumpkin seeds, sunflower seeds, dried fruit and cacao nibs. In separate bowl, whisk together sunflower butter, coconut syrup and sea salt. Pour over nut mixture and fold to evenly distribute ingredients. Batter will be very sticky.

Line a 9 x 12-inch baking dish with parchment paper and spoon in seed mixture. Cover with a second piece of parchment paper and press mixture firmly to evenly fill casserole (this will require some work and muscle). Smooth paper over top of bars so that it sticks on top and refrigerate 2 hours or until firm.

Remove from refrigerator and cut into 18 bars, about 1 x 4½ inches each. Store in airtight container.

Note: If using salted seeds, omit sea salt.

MAKES 18 bars

A FEW OF MY FAVORITE THINGS

This list represents some of the products and resources that I use regularly to support my efforts to eat clean and live well. Access to these and other quality and locally produced items will vary depending on where you live. Create positive change by asking for specific brands you know to be clean, so your grocer can better serve the needs of you and your community.

APPLIANCES, COOKWARE AND KITCHEN TOOLS

BLENDERS (High-Powered)
Blendtec® | blendtec.com
Vitamix™ | vitamix.com

CANNING AND MASON JARS
Ball | freshpreserving.com
Le Parfait® | leparfait.com
Weck | weckjars.com

DEHYDRATORS
Excalibur® | excaliburdehydrator.com

CAST IRON SKILLETS
Lodge® | lodgemfg.com

DUTCH OVENS
Le Creuset® | lecreuset.com
Lodge® | lodgemfg.com

GLASS STORAGE
Pyrex® | pyrex.com

RICE COOKERS
(With stainless steel interior bowl)
Miracle Exclusive™ | miracleexclusives.com

ESSENTIAL OILS

Young Living™ Essential Oils | youngliving.com

FARMS, FARMERS MARKETS AND CSAs

Eat Well Guide | eatwellguide.org
Local Harvest | localharvest.org
USDA | search.ams.usda.gov/farmersmarkets/

FOODSTUFFS

APPLE CIDER VINEGAR
Bragg® | bragg.com

BEANS (Canned)
Eden® | edenfoods.com

BEANS, FLOURS, GRAINS (Packaged)
Ancient Harvest® | ancientharvest.com
Arrowhead Mills | arrowheadmills.com
Bob's Red Mill® | bobsredmill.com
Eden® | edenfoods.com
The Teff Company | theteffco.com
truRoots® | truroots.com

BROWN RICE VINEGAR
Eden® | edenfoods.com

CHOCOLATE
Enjoy Life® | enjoylifefoods.com
Sunspire™ | sunspire.com

COCONUT PRODUCTS
Artisana® | artisanafoods.com
Coconut Secret | coconutsecret.com
Let's Do®…Organic | edwardandsons.com
Nutiva® | nutiva.com
So Delicious® | sodeliciousdairyfree.com
Spectrum® | spectrumorganics.com

A FEW OF MY FAVORITE THINGS

LEMON/LIME JUICE
Santa Cruz Organic® | santacruzorganic.com

LIQUID AMINOS
Bragg® | bragg.com

MAYONNAISE (Grapeseed Oil)
Follow Your Heart® | followyourheart.com

MIRIN
Eden® | edenfoods.com

MISO
South River Miso Company® | southrivermiso.com

NUTRITIONAL YEAST
Bragg® | bragg.com

PASTA (Gluten-Free)
Jovial® | jovialfoods.com
Tinkyáda® | tinkyada.com
truRoots® | truroots.com

SESAME OIL (Toasted and Hot)
Eden® | edenfoods.com

SUPERFOODS
Navitas Naturals® | navitasnaturals.com

TEMPEH
Hosta Hill Fermented Foods | hostahill.com

TOFU
The Bridge | bridgetofu.com

UME PLUM VINEGAR
Eden® | edenfoods.com

VEGETABLE STOCK (Dehydrated)
Seitenbacher® | www.seitenbacher.com

HERBS AND TEAS
Frontier™ Natural Products Co-op | frontiercoop.com
Love and Tea Company | loveandtea.com
Mountain Rose Herbs® | mountainroseherbs com
Starwest® Botanicals | starwest-botanicals.com

NATURAL FOOD CO-OPS
Coop Directory Service | coopdirectory.org
Cooperative Grocer Network | cooperativegrocer.coop
Organic Consumers Association | organicconsumers.org
Organic Store Locator | organicstorelocator.com

PRODUCT INFO AND REVIEWS
Environmental Working Group | ewg.org

SEEDS AND GARDENING SUPPLIES
Baker Creek | rareseeds.com
Fedco Co-op Garden Supplies | fedcoseeds.com
High Mowing Organic Seeds | highmowingseeds.com
Johnny's Selected Seeds | johnnyseeds.com
Seed Savers Exchange | seedsavers.org

WATER FILTERS
Multi-pure® | multipure.com

INDEX

SPRING

....

....

....

....

....

....

....

....

....

....

....

....

....

....

....

....

....

....

SUMMER

....

....

....

....

....

....

....

....

....

....

....

....

....

....

....

....

....

....

FALL

....

....

....

....

....

....

....

....

....

....

....

....

....

....

....

....

....

....

....

WINTER

This book and journey would not be possible without the people in this picture. That is not to suggest that they like every recipe I prepare, always eat clean, are equal participants in our vegetable garden and join me on every farm and farmers market excursion. Rather, they pull me in many directions, sharing their own interests and passions and making life richer as a result. Finding balance can be a challenge, but like eating clean and living well, the process and those I am blessed to share it with are much more important than the end result. This family is my most cherished gift.

Terry

One of the most important relationships we have is with food. Be mindful of your choices and enjoy the nourishment that results from eating clean and living well.